WORLD POVERTY

Challenge and Response

by

Nigel Dower

Lecturer in Logic and Moral Philosophy

University of Aberdeen

William Sessions Limited
The Ebor Press, York
England
1983

ISBN: O 900657 78 2

Note: As this book was going to press, the Brandt Commission
published its second Report *Common Crisis: North-
South - Co-operation for World Recovery*. All refer-
ences to The Brandt Report in the text of Dr. Dower's
book are to the first Report *North-South - A Programme
for Survival* (1980). The sobering message of the
second report confirms however the urgent need for the
spirit of global co-operation and for the values for
which this book argues.

Produced by
Jackson Morley Sessions Limited
53 Low Petergate
YORK
England

CONTENTS

page

Foreword

Preface iii

Part I - Foundations

Chapter 1 The Challenge of World Poverty 1
The Challenge 1; The Basic Argument 2;
Moral Argument and Reform 5; The Brandt
Report 10; Means and Ends 11.

Chapter 2 The Promotion of Good 14
Utilitarianism 14; Assessment of
Utilitarianism 17; The Duty not
to Kill 20.

Chapter 3 Human Rights 24
The Right to Life 24; Rights: Some
Distinctions 25; Human Good 29;
Political, Civil, Economic and
Social Rights 35.

Chapter 4 Social Justice 37
Charity 37; Two Arguments 40;
Basic Needs 42; Rawls' Theory 45.

Part II - Global Issues

Chapter 5 The Third World and The West 51
The Capacity to Help 51; Credit and
Debit 54; A 'conservative' Critique 59;
A 'radical' Critique 62; Forms of
Egalitarianism 64; Inequality: The
Racialist Factor 66; Corrective Justice
and Responsibility 68.

Chapter 6 World Poverty and Western Self-Interest .. 71
Two arguments 71; Genuine Development? 73;
Morality and Self-Interest 74; The Problem
of the Free Rider 76; Self-Interest and
Global Identity 77; The Role of the
Individual 80.

page

Chapter 7   World Poverty and Environment   83
Divergence or convergence? 83;
The 'Back to Nature' approach 84;
Moral One-sidedness 85; The Need
for Global Conservation Strategies 89;
The Just and Sustainable Society 91.

Chapter 8   Resource Scarcity and the Problem of Growth   95
An argument 95; Western Obligation:
Myth or Reality? 100; The Moral Basis
of Optimism 104; The Rejection of
International Obligations 105;
Growth 108.

Chapter 9   Armaments, Violence and World Poverty   ..   115
'The Arms Race Kills' 115; Reasons for
Disarmament 120; Violence 122;
Institutional Violence 126; Omission 129;
Peace and Development 130.

Part III - World Poverty and the Individual

Chapter 10   Actions and Attitudes   133
Collective Responsibility 133;
What can one do? 135; What ought
to be done? 137; Rules, Principles
and Personal Choice 139; Promoting
Justice 142; The Concept of Caring 145;
The Sense of Responsibility 148.

Chapter 11   Have we the Will?   150
How Far are Changes of Attitude
Possible? 150; Three Obstacles 151;
The need for More Knowledge 152;
Caring and Self-Fulfilment 154;
Ideals and Requirements 157;
Self-Interest 159; International
Identity 160.

Notes   164

Bibliography and List of Relevant Organisations   175

Index   177

by SIR GEOFFREY M. WILSON, K.C.B.
Past Chairman of Race Relations Board and
present Chairman of Oxfam

There has been no shortage over the last 20 or 30 years of books, pamphlets, articles and arguments about Third World Poverty and whether the rich world should do anything about it and if so, why? So why yet another book? The answer is that this one really is different. Nigel Dower is a moral philosopher and his primary objective is to defend a moral goal by moral argument and to establish that helping to alleviate world poverty is - like justice - a moral requirement and not just the optional expression of an ideal. So his concern is with basic attitudes rather than with practical action - that will follow if the basic attitudes are right.

Nigel Dower subjects the arguments based on self-interest, charity, power and political relationships to a rigorous examination from the standpoint of a moral philosopher and calls our attention to the moral assumptions which underlie what we like to think of as purely hard-headed practical courses of action. What he does is to establish the case for "foreign aid" - or rather, personal and political involvement in the alleviation of world poverty - on a firm philosophical base of moral obligation instead of on the shifting sands of self-interest and political expediency.

Not everybody will agree with his analysis, but it is an important contribution to the "world poverty" debate and will be warmly welcomed in many quarters.

March 1983   Geoffrey Wilson

A note about the origins of this book may be helpful to the reader. In 1974 I became involved with a local branch of the World Development Movement and a year later also became involved with the United Nations Association. Through these organisations I became concerned about the issues of world poverty, the environment, peace and disarmament, and later started relating these issues to my professional interest in moral philosophy. The publication of the Brandt Report in 1980 stimulated me into conceiving a book on ethics and world poverty, and during the Autumn of that year, when I was kindly granted a term of Sabbatical Leave from the University of Aberdeen, a first draft was written. Much redrafting has occurred since then, though needless to say I am still far from fully satisfied with the result.

This book is written for the general reader who wants to explore the issues raised by our responses in the West to world poverty. It is *not* a textbook in academic philosophy, though it should interest students of philosophy who believe that moral philosophy should descend from its ivory tower and engage with practical issues in the world. It is *not* a book full of economic facts and theories. Clearly some broad economic assumptions are made, but if they are dismissed as wrong or naive, the main purpose of the book would not be undermined at all. Nor is it a book which tells the reader in any detail about developing countries, or about the concrete problems of development in all its diversity. It engages with the relationships between rich and poor countries at a fairly general level, and deals with general moral principles and values, not their detailed applications. In this sense it bears the stamp of a philosopher's mind.

I was once told in effect that books concerned with promoting moral arguments were a bad thing because they simply made people feel guilty - and people were already too guilt-ridden. So let me say that my object is to stimulate people into action and to encourage attitudes of caring, it is not to make people feel guilty. My hope is that people will *want* to respond to the challenge, not that they become divided selves, divided between inclination and duty.

The book makes no religious assumptions. The arguments are essentially secular ones which should make sense to people of good will and reason quite generally. As a member of the Society of Friends (Quakers) I find inspiring the idea that there is 'that of God' in all human beings. Maybe some of the arguments in this book have what strength they have because of this religious assumption below the surface. Maybe too, non-religious people of good will who respond to the arguments are, without realising it, responding to what is essentially a religious idea of the equality and objective importance of all human beings. Be that as it may, my arguments are intended to stand independently of explicit theological or Biblical assumptions. I hope too that they will seem to confirm, rather than challenge, the moral beliefs of religious people of good will whose premisses may be rather different.

My thanks are due to many people. Mary, my wife, has helped in many ways - keeping the children out of the way in the heat of production, encouraging me in my more gloomy moods, advising me where my style becomes more than usually ponderous. I should also like to thank in particular Ronald Avent, Nancy Hare, Rosemary Herdson, David Pearce, Dan Shaw, Scott Styles, Emmett Weir, and Chris Wigglesworth for reading earlier drafts and discussing the issues. I am also grateful to June Patterson, Anne Shade and Irene Thomson for typing assistance. Margot and Bill Sessions, of William Sessions Ltd., have taken more than a mere professional interest in the project, which I have appreciated.

Last but not least, let me thank my parents Jean and Arthur Dower, for their constant interest in this offspring of their offspring. This book is dedicated to them.

Nigel Dower
Aberdeen
August 1982

PART ONE: FOUNDATIONS

Chapter 1

THE CHALLENGE OF WORLD POVERTY

The Challenge

It is estimated that 800 million people live in what is
called 'absolute poverty'.[1] 'Absolute poverty' is a
condition of life which, in the words of Robert MacNamara
of the World Bank, "is so limited by malnutrition,
illiteracy, disease, high infant mortality and low life
expectancy as to be beneath any rational definition of human
decency".[2] The vast majority of the 'absolute poor' live in
most of the countries in Africa, Southern Asia and Latin
America, countries often referred to as 'Developing Countries'
or, collectively, as 'The Third World' or 'The South'. It
is hard for those in the rich North to comprehend or
visualise this kind of poverty. It is *much* worse than the
kind of poverty which we rightly regard as a scandal in the
rich countries of the North. It bears no relation at all to
the relative poverty of a man who struggles to makes ends
meet and who, like Burns' man of 'honest poverty' holds his
head high in self-respecting independence. Absolute poverty
is quite degrading and undermines the possibility of a
reasonable and fulfilling existence. 800 million - a fifth
of the world's population - are in this condition.

Numerous facts and statistics can be mentioned which bear
out this tragic picture. 10,000 people die per day from
lack of nutrition.[3] That is over three and a half million
per year. In developing countries 40% of the people do not
have access to pure water, and this is one of the main
factors accounting for widespread disease in poor countries.[4]
300 million people, mainly in the Third World, are unemployed
or seriously underemployed. We are rightly concerned about
our own high unemployment percentages, but they are nevertheless low compared with the global average of 35%.[5] In
many poorer countries there are no unemployment benefits
either. Another feature of poverty is lack of education:
there are still 34 countries in the world where over 80%
of the people are illiterate.[4]

These are just a few manifestations of the extent and
character of absolute poverty. It is also important to

1

stress its *relative* character as well - that is, relative to
the wealth of the rich nations. The average income *per
capita* in Developing countries was, in 1975, approximately
$ 441, that of Western countries $ 4831.[3] The difference,
which has become no smaller since, is in the ration of *over
1 to 10*. Average life expectancy in developing countries is
about forty two, that in Western countries about seventy
two.[6] The richest 30% of the world's people consume 75% of
the world's non-renewable resources.[7] One example of the
effect of the difference in wealth is given by Ronald Sider
in *Rich Christians in an Age of Hunger,* when he considers
the fact that in the USA 17% of disposable income is spent
on food, but in India 67%:

> If one is spending 17 per cent of one's disposable income
> on food, a 50 per cent increase in food costs is an
> irritation. But if one is already spending 67 per cent
> of one's income on food to buy just enough to live on, a
> 50 per cent increase means starvation.[8]

Facts like these show quite clearly that relatively speaking
we in the West are *very* well off, even though there are areas
of appalling poverty here as well. Once this fact is coupled
with the absolute character of world poverty, it is surely
obvious that we ought to do a lot to alleviate world poverty.
Since such poverty is an evil which just is not to be
tolerated, then we who are affluent ought to do what we can
to tackle it. For even if our affluence is reduced in so
doing - which it may not be - it cannot be argued that what
we lost can in any way be weighed against what is to be
gained. Being less rich is not *an evil not to be tolerated*
in the way that absolute poverty is. It is not a case of
simply weighing up our *interest* in being affluent with their
interest in not being very poor, for the two are not morally
commensurable. To think of the problem simply in terms of
an 'interest versus interest' model would be to distort the
whole issue.

It may be asked: What makes extreme poverty an evil which
ought not to be tolerated? If it is not to be tolerated,
why ought we in *one* country to be concerned with removing
evils which exist in *other* countries? Briefly the answers
to be given, are as follows.

The Basic Argument

(a) One should accept as a fundamental principle the

2

principle of promoting human good. Human good is, in principle, wherever it may be achieved or maintained, something that ought to be promoted by those who can do so. In particular it is especially important that the conditions which most seriously mar human existence should be removed by those who are able to do so. For the worse a person's condition, the more pressing is action to improve it. On this basis it is clear that the lot of many millions of 'absolute poor' deserves our practical attention.

This principle is based on a fundamental and universal fact about human beings and what is needed for their well-being. There is, that is, a basic moral 'right to life' and the conditions necessary for it. No distinction is made between human beings in different countries. If we respond to the principle it is appropriate to be concerned with the poor of the Third World, just because they are very poor and we have the capacity to help them. In practice of course there are qualifications to be made, since numerous other considerations must enter into one's policies and decisions. But if the extremity of poverty together with our own affluence are properly appreciated, then acceptance of the principle should result in a general attitude of concern for the poor in the Third World. This attitude, if generally developed, would not only lead to a much wider sense of *private* commitment in people, but would also influence their electoral preferences and thus make possible or necessary much greater *public* commitment to the Third World in the form of both Aid programmes and a willingness to see reforms in the international economic system.

(b)   The second kind of argument takes as its starting point the conception of morality as a system of rules and institutions which serve everyone's interests in a society and which can be thought of as agreed principles of social co-operation. This conception is then extended to the international or trans-national sphere: where there are extensive or substantial relationships between countries, these basic rules and principles have application in the relationships between countries. The idea of fully international community or society may seem strange, and certainly few people have a proper 'sense' of it. Yet the facts which prompt the use of the phrase are there for all to see - extensive economic relationships, ecological interdependence and so on. And certainly there is well developed in or between certain areas or regions of the world the sense as well as the reality of what may be called trans-national community of society. The onus is then on the sceptics to show why the principles of morality should *not* apply to relations between different countries and their members. However this cannot be shown.

There are many areas in which an established and developed system of international morality is called for. There are two particular features however which are relevant to our theme. First, there should be principles of fair dealing in economic transactions, which should act as a curb on the tendency for the economically powerful to impose trading arrangements to their benefit. It would be quite disingenuous of Western businessmen or Government agents to be regarded as exempt, wholly or partly, from normal considerations of justice in their dealings with those from a developing country. The very existence of trading relations establishes the relevant degree of 'trans-national' society, and belies any excuse that the normal rules of fair dealing do not apply in this kind of situation. The point can be added that economic practices can be criticised on this ground, quite apart from the effect of such practices in causing poverty or preventing effective measures from being taken against poverty.

The other argument which relates directly to poverty is this. One feature of living in a community or society which is commonly accepted by people of nearly all political persuasions is that a society or community should *care* for those who fall into desperate need. It is the responsibility of a society so far as it is able to prevent extreme poverty or to rescue people from extreme hardships. How far this caring should be done by individuals, private organisations or by the State from welfare provision and other measures is a matter for debate, but the general idea that society is collectively responsible for serving basic needs is commonly accepted.

This responsibility should be seen as a requirement of 'social justice', and one which should be extended into the international sphere. For it is clear, in the case of most developing countries in relation to the West, that the extensive interconnections establish the necessary features

4

for an enlarged concept of community or society. It is
where these ideas of international society or community have
significant application, that the idea of social justice has
application.

Thus we can say that, given the fact that developing countries
are not in a position to deal with poverty adequately themselves, it is a requirement of international social justice
that we should assist in the process of development. If we
look at matters in this light, we can see Government Aid,
not as an act of charity, but as part of the 'tax' paid by
richer countries to be used to alleviate poverty in poorer
countries - just as the rich pay taxes which are used to
finance the welfare services within Western countries. Indeed
it is this idea of international social justice which underlies the Brandt Commission's recommendation that there should
be an international system of taxation on international
activities such as trading, where such taxation would be
used to finance development schemes.[9]

Moral Argument and Reform

The preceding arguments for what may be called the 'central
proposition', that we have a substantial obligation to help
alleviate world poverty, will be developed in the next few
chapters. Several doubts may however be raised about the
whole exercise. How far can moral argument take us in
practical terms? Will moral argument really make any
difference to what individuals, institutions or governments
do? If someone assumes that the answers to these questions
must be 'not much' or 'not at all', then clearly this book
is not for him, unless he happens to be fascinated by moral
arguments which he believes to be ineffective. For the book
is written in the conviction that, properly understood and
developed, moral arguments can exercise a powerful influence
not only in leading to positive action but also in guiding
the ways in which we allow ourselves to pursue our interests.

The perspective of the book will be resisted by at least two
sorts of thinkers.[10] Those who tend to belong to the
political 'Right' may make two claims in parallel. First,
social, political and economic relationships are essentially
controlled by self-interest - the only possible exception
being personal relationships - and by the sectional interests
of groups, such as business companies, professional associa-
tions, Trades Unions, or by the national interests of countries

5

and governments. Second, since there is really no alternative to such patterns of human relationships, it is perfectly
legitimate for individuals, groups or countries to pursue
their interests. The total situation may be made more
attractive by occasional or sustained acts of generosity -
by private charity or public aid - but there is nothing
wrong with the basic patterns of power relations. 'Free
Market' Capitalism, whether national or international, is
to be accepted. For as far as the interests of most people
are concerned, nothing is to be gained and much lost in the
centrally planned economies of communist states which are
no more than differently arranged patterns of power
relationships.

On this 'conservative' view any kind of moral argument which
does not endorse the basic legitimacy of the pursuit of
self-interest at individual, institutional or national
levels, can be regarded as being unrealistic because it is
not firmly secured in the dynamics of human relationships;
or dangerous because it may inspire people to disrupt the
social order.

On the other hand, the perspective of the book may come
under attack from those on the political 'Left'. Those on
the Left may share one of the assumptions of those on the
Right - that human relationships are generally controlled
by sectional and national interests. Only they will claim
that there *is* an alternative to this, namely the Socialist,
Marxist or Communist Order. This Order however will only
come about by the concerted efforts of some revolutionary
group which must use political muscle and military force to
wrest wealth and power from those in control. Once this has
been achieved however, the typical patterns of power
relationships will give way to a new social order of harmony
and greater human fulfilment.

On this 'radical' view, it will do no good addressing moral
arguments to those individuals, groups or governments who
now happen to be wealthy, privileged or generally advantaged.
They will never be *persuaded* to change anything so that other
groups or countries benefit. Rational argument about what
is right or in everyone's longterm interests will have no
effect. Those in power will only be 'persuaded' by force
and the calculations of self-interest which arise when they
are threatened. Capitalism, whether national or

international, is totally unacceptable and must be destroyed, along with that sort of democracy which supports it. It cannot be improved or rendered acceptable by the veneer of Aid programmes or the generosity of individuals. These salve the conscience but solve nothing.

This book attempts a 'middle way' between these two approaches. Its approach might be called the 'reforming' approach. There is, it is argued, significant scope for change based on moral arguments and appeals to enlightened self-interest (i.e. self-interest not based on threats from another group). It *is* worth addressing such arguments to those who are better off or powerful, whether as individuals, or in institutions or government. Part of what is meant by the human capacity for rationality is our *moral reasonableness* - our susceptibility to the force of certain types of thinking about ourselves which transcend appeals to immediate self-interest. It is of course to be granted that much in social political and economic relationships is determined in the ways which the conservative and radical approaches emphasise, but it is 'much' not 'all' or 'almost all'. Nor is it a fixed constant of the human condition. In some conditions power and self-interest no doubt predominate, in other conditions moral reasonableness may have a significant influence. If the radical thinks that such conditions as the latter will come through force and revolution, the reformer thinks that they are more likely to come through rational persuasion and evolution.

Part of the 'middle way' adopted here involves refusing to adopt an attitude of either blanket acceptance or blanket condemnation of capitalism. Capitalism should be reformed not thrown out, transformed from within rather than attacked from outside. Nevertheless there are many things done in the name of Capitalism and many attitudes associated with Capitalism which need to be criticised. Many fundamental reforms need to be all, for instance, in the international economic system, and also in the internal economic practices of some developing countries themselves. On the other hand, the practice of Communism, which is usually taken to be 'the other' way of conducting economic activity, does not commend itself as a superior alternative. Though it is certainly necessary that there should be extensive 'regulation' of capitalist economies and that certain 'redistributive'

7

measures to help alleviate poverty should be built into the working of an economic system, this is a far cry from a centrally planned economy. Indeed there is little to commend in the models of centrally planned economies, either as models of how Western Industrial economies ought to be run, or as models of how the international economy ought to be run. Apart from their inherent tendencies towards inefficiency and burdensome bureaucracy, they seem naturally if not inevitably, conjoined with authoritarian government and the suppression of civil and political liberties.

With regard to the internal economic arrangements of developing countries themselves, the situation is less clear. It is likely that what is appropriate for developing countries will rarely be a blueprint Capitalist model or a blueprint Socialist model, but rather models which combine elements of both and extend them in directions appropriate to local circumstances, indigenous values and cultural traditions. The situations in different countries will vary considerably: so too will their socio-economic responses. Thus it may be that in some countries the power of the wealthy is so entrenched and there is such resistance to change, that only a change in the socio-economic system towards a socialist or communist regime will enable the poor to improve their position. On the other hand in many other countries there may be progress towards development for the poor within a broadly capitalist framework, provided adequate checks and balances are introduced and the democratic rights of minority groups are properly protected.

The remarks of the last paragraph illustrate a general point. There are certainly elements of radicalism in the arguments of this book. But this radicalism does not belong to the left side of the conventional socio-political spectrum from Socialist/Communist to Conservative/Capitalist. It rather stems from a critical stance which questions many of the assumptions *shared* by all shades of political opinion within the capitalist democratic framework as well as by much economic thinking in Communist countries - for instance the commitment to ever increasing material affluence and the assumption of the inevitablility and desirability of 'big' organisations. (Another respect in which this book may be seen as 'radical' is its insistence on an

8

internationalist perspective rather than a nationalistic perspective: again this cuts right across the conventional Right/Left spectrum.)

This new if quiet radicalism was of course given eloquent expression by the late E. F. Schumacher in *Small is Beautiful* and other writings.[11] It is partly in the light of this kind of radicalism that one can be deeply critical of much in the capitalist landscape, without believing that we have to hand a preferable fully fledged alternative. For all its imperfections, we live with the capitalist system in our own countries and in the international system, and whilst the ideal and no doubt eventually realisable model of socio-economic existence is neither capitalist nor socialist, it is more appropriate to work within the present capitalist system in order to improve or reform it, than to work to destroy it. For the product of such destruction would be even worse.

It is worth observing that in the international sphere investments and loans made by national governments or by international institutions such as the World Bank are, in an important sense, as much capitalist enterprises as are the investments of large trans-national corporations. Thus by this token a country with a centrally planned economy which pursues an investment policy in another country, is engaging in a capitalist enterprise. This fact does not serve to condone - or condemn - the investment policies of govern-ments, but simply illustrates the point that so long as you have autonomous nation-states, there will be a significant degree of 'free market' in the international system. Only if you had a world government which decided - and it would not necessarily so decide - to impose the equivalent of a centrally planned economy upon the whole world, would international capitalism be finally removed. Such a development in the foreseeable future is neither feasible nor desirable.

Meantime what is important is that there be introduced, through concerted international effort, the kinds of checks and balances and the degree of control and planning which are commonly accepted as being essential and useful within the internal capitalist economies of Western industrialised countries. In particular greater international control, through the development of international law, is needed to

curb the less acceptable activities of transnational
companies. However we should clearly recognise that, unless
we think that Western economic involvement in developing
countries is altogether a bad thing for them, transnationals
also have an immensely positive role to play in development
as well. It is a matter for great regret that in the North-
South 'Dialogue' of recent years, the South's demand for a
'New International Economic Order' has been seen by the
North, and sometimes presented by the South, as a threat to
the Capitalist system itself.[12] It is really nothing of the
kind. Rather the 'NIEO' is essentially a programme for
modifying and stabilising the international capitalist
economic system so as to give greater benefits to the poorer
nations, and, if the Brandt Commission is right, to the
richer nations as well.

The Brandt Report

Indeed the reforming approach taken here reflects in a
general way the approach of the Brandt Commission Report.
This Report on the world economy produced by a high-powered
and independent commission and published at the beginning of
1980 argues that in order to tackle contructively the problem
of world poverty and also to revitalise the ailing world
economy, it is essential to reform the international economic
institutions and make massive transfers of financial
assistance to poor countries. The report gives two basic
reasons for its proposals: first, it is a matter of morality,
of what it sometimes calls compassion, sometimes social
justice, that the Rich Nations act, and second, it is a
matter of enlightened self-interest for them so to act. With
regard to the latter argument, the Report offers the positive
argument (the 'carrot') that development in poor countries
will stimulate Western exports, and the negative argument
(the 'stick') that unless the economic system is reformed,
the world economy will collapse.[13]

There are many detailed respects in which this Report can be
and has been rightly criticised, but it remains, at least
for anyone who is not so conservative as to reject all change
or so radical as to reject all attempts at reform, an
important and influential statement of the philosophy of
reform and non-coercive persuasion. As Barbara Ward said in
one of her last speeches, "When you come down to the last
analysis of the Brandt Report, it is its belief in community,

its belief in mankind, its belief that we can work together..." that is the important thing.[14] The moral tone of the work is reflected in the frequent reference to ideas like compassion, humanity, social justice, basic rights, human solidarity and international community. But these ideas are appealed to, they are not developed. Their potency is no doubt assumed in a work largely devoted to the empirical facts and to detailed and technical proposals.

For many people however these ideas simply are not accepted as serious bases for commitment to action. It is easy to acknowledge the words, but then do nothing about it. For there are a number of subterfuges which one can engage in, whether consciously or unconsciously. It is easy to let oneself believe that what happens beyond one's country's border does not *really* count, or count all that much; that international morality is not *real* in the sense that the morality of one's own society is real. It is easy to think of the ideas of compassion, justice and community as expressions of an idealism which can be disregarded in practice. It is easy to think that caring - particularly for those at a distance from one - is not really a duty at all, and that one's moral responsibility really ends with what one positively does or aims at, and does not extend to the effects of one's *non*-involvement and indifference.

These and other temptations to find excuses need to be resisted - we will come across them again and again in the course of discussion. So the claim that the ideas of compassion, justice and human rights are powerful ideas cannot be left undefended. It needs careful elaboration and defence. This is what is attempted in this book, and in this respect the book can be regarded as a kind of footnote to the Brandt Report.

Means and Ends

The primary objective of the book then is to defend a moral goal by moral argument. It is important to note what this implies. The book is concerned with *ends,* rather than with means, with the central proposition that we ought to help, rather than with the wide variety of ways in which one can help. It is important to note that 'help' is used here, and in the course of this book, in a very wide sense. The phrase 'help combat/alleviate/tackle world poverty' is intended to

11

cover *any* course of action, policy or approach which does contribute to the objective of reducing world poverty. What is often thought of as 'helping' others - such as charitable giving - is only a small part of the wide range of things that both can be done and ought to be done, and indeed in some circumstances may not really 'help' or be appropriate at all.

It is not then the purpose of this book to examine all the detailed ways and means which are available to individuals, groups or governments, or to set them in some rank order of importance. Some thinkers will stress the orthodox means called Aid along with private charity, some see the need for international economic reform, some stress the need for internal economic reforms within developing countries, some emphasise the role of education, some stress the avoidance of protectionist measures against Third World imports, some stress the role of the United Nations and of international agencies, such as Unicef, F.A.O., W.H.O., U.N.D.P. and The World Bank.

All these suggestions and many others have relevance and it is narrow-minded to opt for just one or two preferred 'solutions' or strategies. Nevertheless there is much careful and patient work that has been done and still needs to be done in examining just what are the most effective things to be done, given that different situations require different solutions. Clearly such work is of vital importance, both for the primary reason that effective development programmes require it, and also for the secondary reason that the publication of such work and its results may help to curb the cynicism which is commonly voiced concerning Aid and other measures aimed at alleviating poverty.

Vitally important as such detailed investigation into 'means' is, it is not what this book is primarily about. Questions about ends are equally vital. Unless we are *fully* committed to the objective of reducing world poverty or pursuing development,[15] we will not have the will to find the way, or rather the range of ways which are open to us. If readers of this book are sceptical about the ways of tackling world poverty which are revealed in the course of the discussion, I would naturally be sorry, - but nothing like as sorry as I would be if readers rejected the importance of the end or objective and thus failed to work out other means which they

12

thought more effective.

It is perhaps an overstatement to say that where there is a will there is a way. For it is no doubt true that means and ends stand in a dynamic two-way relationship to each other. On the one hand, where there is a strong commitment to an end, a person will take the necessary means, or if they are not available, *search* for them. On the other hand, the persistent lack of effective means - or means that do not involve high 'costs' of various kinds - may dull or destroy commitment, whilst the knowledge that means are readily available may convert mere interest in a possible end into firm commitment. So it is perhaps important to say that the argument does partly rest upon the assumption that there is a wide range of things that *can be* done to help with development in the Third World. Whether they *will be* done, is sadly, another matter. That they *ought to be* done is the thesis of this book.

Chapter 2

THE PROMOTION OF GOOD

In this and the following two chapters the philosophical basis for the central proposition that we have a substantial obligation to help alleviate world poverty will be examined. It is useful first of all to consider several kinds of moral argument which overstate the case. That is, they would establish, if they were correct, not merely that we had a substantial obligation, but also that we had an all-pervasive or relentless obligation. In examining what is right about these views and what is wrong about them we will begin to establish a sound basis for our thesis.

Utilitarianism

It is useful to start by looking at a well-known theory called Utilitarianism. The basic idea behind this doctrine is very simple. It is that there is *one* fundamental moral principle, namely the principle of promoting human good to the greatest extent possible. The theory is best known in its Classical formulation, which is associated with the writings of the nineteenth century philosophers Jeremy Bentham[1] and John Stuart Mill.[2] Their doctrine was that one ought to promote the *greatest happiness,* though sometimes the longer phrase 'the greatest happiness of the greatest number' was used. The essential feature of the Classical formulation was that the ultimate justification for any action, including such actions as following rules, enacting legislation and supporting - or opposing - social institutions, was that, compared with any other action which the agent could have performed, that action produced the greatest amount of happiness. If it did that, it was right, if it did not, then it was wrong.

In calculating the consequences of an action, one must of course take into account all the negative aspects as well as the positive aspects, all the pain, suffering or unhappiness which would be involved as well as all the pleasure, joy or happiness. In fact, happiness was given a *hedonistic* interpretation, i.e. an interpretation in terms of pleasure and pain. Now many Utilitarians would question this identification of happiness with pleasure. They might prefer to think of it in terms of the satisfaction of desires or the successful pursuit of one's interests. Others again would prefer to claim that what constitutes *good,* and hence what one ought to be concerned with promoting as much as possible, is not usefully identified with happiness as such.

But what would be agreed upon by these thinkers is that the supreme moral principle is concerned with maximising good. This ultimately is what morality is all about. This claim however is not generally intended as a *descriptive* claim. It is not claimed that this principle underlies the actual moral thinking of all or even most human beings. For it is obvious that many people would, if they reflected upon the basis of their moral outlook, no doubt acknowledge a plurality of principles and values which they would not see as all deriving from one central principle such as the Utilitarian principle. Rather Utilitarianism is generally a *normative* claim. It is the claim that if we think rationally about morality we will see the appropriateness of the Utilitarian principle, and reject other views as the products of superstition, muddle-headedness, tradition or sheer rule-worship.[3] Utilitarians do not, I hasten to add, reject the following of rules, for instance rules about not stealing or not breaking promises. For the following of rules generally is in accordance with the supreme principle, and there is also a Utilitarian justification for teaching and enforcing well-established rules. But to follow a rule without such a justifying background, would indeed be sheer rule-worship and be quite irrational.

There is some appeal to this doctrine. One way of seeing its appeal is to reflect on the following line of thought.

(i) The 'moral point of view' is, in essence, the antithesis of egoism, i.e. of being concerned with and finding value in one's own good alone. It is thus concerned with the good of others, or, to be more accurate, the good of any human being, including oneself. It is not concerned with the good merely of *some* others, but with the good of *any* other person. That is, anyone's good is, in principle, something to be promoted, and to be promoted by anyone who is in a position to do so.

(ii) Furthermore, if one rejects the egoist standpoint, it is clear that the good of one person is of no more importance than that of any other person. One cannot argue, for instance, that the good of some other person is, in principle, of less importance or of less objective value than that of

15

another, because he is, for instance, unknown to one, is of different nationality, has a different religious faith or has a different racial origin.

(iii) If one acknowledges that one ought to promote the good of others, it is an intuitively obvious corollary that one ought to promote it as much as possible. For what possible rational grounds are there for stopping short of accepting the principle that one ought to promote the maximum amount of good? If one then interprets 'good' in terms of happiness, one gets the Classical Utilitarian formulation of the supreme principle of morality.

There are many variations or interpretations of Utilitarianism which we need not go into.[4] What needs to be brought out is the fact that if this principle is taken seriously, it has quite radical consequences for our decisions and policies in relation to world poverty, and indeed in relation to many other social problems. For if our concern is to maximise happiness or human well-being, we will spend our time and use our resources to just that end and no other. And we will do so all the time. For to do otherwise would be to contravene the supreme principle of morality. No one who weighed this proposition seriously could avoid drawing the conclusion that a vast amount could be done and would be done if this principle were consistently applied, compared with what people, even generous and socially minded people, actually do. A single-minded application of this principle would be quite revolutionary in its consequences.[5]

The revolutionary character of these practical consequences can be tempered, but not eliminated, by the following qualifications which a Utilitarian would undoubtedly wish to add. (i) It is no doubt true that whilst the good of *all* men is, in principle, to be promoted and to be regarded as having equal value, in practice of course the area in which one can be most effective in promoting good is often very restricted. One is often better placed to promote good or, on its negative side, prevent harm, pain or frustration, in relation to friends, neighbours, relatives or those with whom one interacts in face-to-face situations, than in relation to those with whom one is only indirectly connected, for instance, through economic relations. So it will often turn out that, when one considers which course of action maximises good, the tangible and identifiable good or

16

removeable harm of some particular others outweighs the less
tangible and more marginal good done to a larger number of
unidentified people, such as would be the object of giving
to some Third World charity.

But it will often turn out that this is not so, usually in
situations where the good of other particular people is not
at issue, or at least not crucially so. What about all the
free time one has, which one could devote to working for
some social cause like world poverty, instead of pottering
in the garden, playing football or reading a novel? What
about all the money one earns or saves, much of which could
be donated to social ends?

(ii) The last point leads into the second qualification.
It is after all to be recognised that the one person whose
good one is most directly in control of is oneself! In
practical terms it will often, from a Utilitarian point of
view be right to attend therefore to the good of oneself.
Thus in practice if a man's good partly consists in certain
relaxations, games, hobbies, cultural activities and so on,
then he ought sometimes to engage in them. If a man's good
presupposes that he has sufficient material means both for
the present and for the future, then his providing this
through work, looking after his things or saving for the
future is something which he ought to some extent to do.

However the qualifications 'sometimes' and 'to some extent'
are important. For such activities as private relaxations,
saving for the future, or indeed indulging one's affections
towards one's family or friends, are only right in just
those situations where *more* good is done thereby than in
any other way. Otherwise they are simply wrong. And surely
honest reflection would reveal that much of what is commonly
regarded as legitimate 'private' pursuits would turn out to
be wrong on the Utilitarian principle. It should be noted
that these remarks do not show that the Utilitarian principle
is either right or wrong. Rather they indicate that this
would be the practical consequence of any forthright
application of that principle.

Assessment of Utilitarianism

Since it is indeed my contention that we ought to be doing
a lot more than we generally do towards alleviating world
poverty, or for that matter other social problems in our own

country, it would be very convenient if one could simply endorse Utilitarianism as a basic moral theory, and let the practical consequences flow from it. Unfortunately, Utilitarianism as a moral theory just will not do. To be sure, it rests upon an acceptable foundation. Of the three points made earlier in order to indicate its appeal, points (i) and (ii) seem to be important and correct. For the good of any person is in principle of equal value and ought to be promoted by others. This expresses a basic *attitude* of concern or caring, which it is the mark of moral maturity to possess. Nevertheless where Utilitarianism goes seriously wrong is over step (iii), that is over the claim that the one principle of morality is the *maximisation* of good. There have been many objections to this principle, but two of them are worth focussing on here. One claims that the principle mis-states moral obligation, the other that it overstates them.

The most common objection to Utilitarianism centres on the fact that it fails to give adequate weight to the demands of justice. We have certain firm intuitions or 'considered judgments' about what is just, and these judgments come into conflict in certain cases with what the Utilitarian principle would require. For instance, it is one thing to maximise good, it is quite another to distribute it fairly. Again, it is one thing to promote the overall good of most people, quite another to respect the rights or liberties of individuals or minority groups.[6] An example of this often given concerns punishment: justice, it is argues, requires that only the guilty be punished and proportionally to their crimes, whereas Utilitarianism, looking only *forward* to consequences, might on occasion require disproportionate punishment, or even punishment of someone known not to be guilty. The fact that these conflicts occur does not of course show that Utilitarianism is wrong: it might be that these intuitions about justice are wrong. But if, as it seems reasonable to suppose, these judgments concerning justice are generally sound and not-to-be-given-up, the upshot is that the Utilitarian principle has to be rejected.

Whilst many thinkers would agree that the independent status of justice - and indeed of other moral values as well - shows the inadequacy of Utilitarianism as a 'one supreme principle of morality' doctrine, there may be considerable disagreement about what these values are and how they are to be interpreted. In particular there are disputes about what the principles of justice are. The way one interprets justice makes a big difference to whether appeals to justice do or do not strengthen commitment to tackling world poverty. For instance, if one makes central to the idea of justice such things as the *liberty* of individuals or corporations to act as they please, the cause of world development will be done no good at all. But if, as is attempted later, one emphasises in the name of justice the right to life or principles of non-exploitative economic relationships, the cause of world development will be served well.

In the light of the above criticism, one could modify the Utilitarian doctrine and think of it not as one supreme principle, but as one of the principles of morality along-side those of justice and maybe others. One might argue, for instance, that within the constraints of justice, one ought to produce as much good or happiness as possible. But so modified, Utilitarianism runs into the second objection which it faces in any case in its main formulation. This objection is that it overstates the nature of our obliga-tions. For it has the consequence that at no time in anyone's life is there any relief from doing one's duty, i.e. from maximising good. The whole of one's life is one long continuous exercise of moral responsibility: for at any given moment one is either doing what one ought to be doing, or one is not, in which case one is in the moral wrong.

Like other moral theories, as we shall see, of the 'as much as you can' variety, it turns the ideals of sainthood and heroism into the demands of duty, and it is counter-intuitive in two respects. First, it allows no 'moral space'. That is, it allows no neutral area in which what one does, for pleasure for instance or in pursuit of one's interests, is *neither* required *nor* ruled out from the moral point of view. For anything one does is, according to the theory, either one's duty or wrong. And second, it does not allow for morally good acts, of great kindness, self-sacrifice or heroism, which lie beyond the requirements of duty: for there is no 'beyond'. Certainly kindness, self-sacrifice and heroism may sometimes be morally required. More generally we ought to help others rather more than we usually acknowledge. But it would be odd to destroy altogether the distinction between such acts of 'supererogation' and the ordinary requirements of morality - even if those requirements turn out to be rather more than are ordinarily recognised.

The general point which emerges from this objection is that a life dominated by omnipresent duty would be a caricature of what a valuable life is like, and is quite false to our understanding of moral experience. Human good consists partly, but significantly and essentially, of certain kinds of activities, relationships and experiences which are thought of as intrinsically worthwhile. We engage in them because we *want* to, because they are subjectively valuable to us, and *not because* by so doing we do our duty, maximise good, promote justice or otherwise respond to the objective demands of our morality.

The point being made here is not the common one that Utilitarianism would require us to be calculating consequences all the time - hardly a self-fulfilling activity! The Utilitarian can answer that point by arguing that we can rely on rules of thumb in much ordinary activity. But the related point is rather that on the Utilitarian hypothesis we must regard whatever we do through the filter of duty, and that this way of looking at the whole of one's life would absolutely sap the vitality of life. It would be a travesty of human wellbeing to try to turn all our reasons for action into requirements of morality. On the other hand this point is no charter for amoralists! For moral consciousness as *one* of the central aspects of one's life is vitally important for the quality of life. Just as with salt, too much of it or none of it can spoil a dish, so with moral consciousness and the quality of life. (Many people take their life under-salted!)

The Duty not to Kill

Let us now look at a most specific and forthright argument given by John Harris in *Violence and Responsibility*[7] and also suggested by Ted Honderich in his lecture 'Our Omissions and their Violence' in *Violence for Equality*.[8] Both these writers are concerned to deny that there is any significant moral difference between a positive action and an omission (failing or refraining), where the results of the two are the same. Thus if I were morally responsible for causing a given harm x, then I would be equally responsible for omitting to do what would have prevented x from happening, given that I could have done so.

Suppose then that we accept the proposition that one ought not to kill human beings. It does not matter for the purpose of this argument whether one accepts this as a pacifist would as an absolute prohibition, or one thinks of it as an important principle to which only certain clear exceptions may be made, e.g. cases of self-defence or fighting in a just war. If then it is wrong to kill human beings, is it not equally wrong to let human beings die who would not have died had one acted in certain ways in which one could have acted? Where is the moral difference between killing a man and failing to prevent him from dying? If you have £100 in the bank and decide to keep it for some private purpose rather than send it to Oxfam, it is almost certain that one person, and highly probably that rather more than one person somewhere in the Third World will shortly die, who would have lived if you had given the money to Oxfam. For your donation would have meant some extension somewhere of an inoculation programme, a sanitation scheme, a health education project, a food handout in a famine area or something else which made that vital (*sic*) difference.

It is worth pointing out that if the argument works, it does not just work for killing and letting die. Take for instance the moral principle, which few would question, that one ought not to cause harm or suffering to fellow human beings. (Again there are exceptions which do not affect the argument). Does it not follow, by a parallel argument, that one ought not to let happen or continue to happen any harm or suffering which one can prevent from happening or from continuing to happen?[9]

What then are we to make of these arguments? Let us be quite clear that the practical consequences of them are fairly dramatic. For if there really is *no* moral difference between killing and letting die and between harming and letting harm occur or continue, it turns out that it is one's duty not merely to refrain from killing or causing harm on the rare occasions when one might want to do so, but also to refrain from omitting to do what one can to prevent deaths and suffering. But the occasions on which it is in one's power to do the latter are not rare at all. Indeed they exist virtually all the time, for rarely are we *not* in a position to *initiate* a course of action which would lead to the prevention of suffering or death. The duty to prevent all the deaths and all the suffering that one can is, given the realities of the world, in practice an inexhaustible one. So the upshot is that the preceding argument yields an 'as much as you can' type of moral doctrine. So if the earlier objection to Utilitarianism is sound, the same objection will apply to the present doctrine. And it is surely counterintuitive to suppose that it is one's duty to do all one can all the time to prevent death and suffering. Saying it is counterintuitive does not of course prove that it is wrong, for one's intuitions may be mistaken. But it does suggest that something is not quite right.

On the other hand, the argument does point in the right direction. For clearly we do have a duty to prevent death and suffering, and the duty to alleviate world poverty is one important application of this central idea. Furthermore there is something which we can call 'negative responsibility'.[10] That is, we can in principle be held responsible for the consequences of omissions. Anyone who accepts as one kind of moral duty the duty of kindness or benevolence implicitly acknowledges this fact. For if it is one's duty to act benevolently, then it is one's duty to refrain from omitting to respond to someone's need. The language of benevolence is different but the point is at bottom the same. And it is surely correct to say that someone who lacks an adequate sense of negative responsibility lacks an important dimension to mature moral awareness.

So how does the argument outlined overstate the case? To go into this properly would require a lengthy examination of the logic of omissions which is immensely complicated, but several brief observations will serve here. First, there is one difference between typical cases of killing and typical cases of letting die. Whereas with killing the death of someone is what is aimed at or intended - either as an end or as a necessary means to an end - with 'letting die' the death of other people is neither what one aims at as an end - one does not want them to die - nor is it a means to some other end. It is simply an unwanted and often unthought of consequence of one's pursuing other objectives. Such objectives might be saving money for the future, spending it on one's children's toys, repairing the house or simply enjoying oneself. Some readers may recognise an allusion here to traditional Catholic doctrine of 'double effect', and there is certainly something in the view that there is a morally significant difference between what one intends or aims at and what one merely forsees as a consequence of what one does.

But it is important not to overdo the distinction. One cannot argue that because a consequence is unintended i.e. not the object of one's intention, it makes *no* difference to the moral value of the proposed course of action. If the foreseen but unwanted consequence is bad enough, it may transform the whole situation. Nevertheless there is some kind of difference of evaluation. There is something morally worse about *intending that someone be dead* (whether by active killing or by failing to save him where no other help is available) than about intending something else, which happens to have the possible or certain consequence that someone dies. But there may for all that be something pretty bad about the latter intention if one has knowledge of that consequence. The general point that needs to be made is that when omissions are and when omissions are not wrong is a matter for detailed investigation. That they are always wrong cannot simply be read off from the simple parallel with positive acts. How far then do we have a negative responsibility to prevent or reduce harm and suffering by our active intervention? The answer to these questions emerge as the rest of the moral arguments are given, though the quick answer might be given: 'Much further than we generally suppose'.

Our discussion has shown that Utilitarianism and the attempt to extend the principle of not killing or causing harm into the negative sphere both overstate the nature of our duty, since neither would allow any moral space in our lives. But they do serve to shake us out of any complacency that if we are not actively causing harm or death then there is nothing morally to be criticised in our behaviour. For an important part of our moral responsibilities lies in how we respond to the needs of others. If 'promoting human good' is seen, not as a maximising principle, but as an unspecific principle expressing an attitude of openness to the welfare of others, it is an important principle. If it is properly understood, it will make a big difference to what we do.

23

Chapter 3

HUMAN RIGHTS

The Right to Life

If we have a general obligation to promote good and to give
assistance where help is needed, what makes it particularly
important that we assist with development in the Third World?
A simple answer to this question was already suggested in
Chapter 1: the combination of the absolute poverty of the
world's poor with the relative affluence of the rich North
provides the basis for claiming that we should help them.
Can we however show more fully why these facts generate a
significant obligation? Perhaps we will locate an appropriate
basis for an argument in the idea of a fundamental *right* to
the conditions necessary for a tolerable life. The idea of
a basic right may provide the weight needed to show how the
alleviation of absolute poverty makes a significant moral
demand on us.

Let us take it as a fundamental premise of our moral thinking
that each human being has a right to life. Let us recognise
two aspects to this. First, there is the right not be
deprived of life by being killed. Second, there is the right
to the conditions essential for one to live, i.e. continue
living. Let us also interpret the right to life in a stronger
rather than a weaker sense. In the weaker sense 'life' means
mere living existence or being biologically alive, but in
the stronger sense 'life' means something like 'a qualitatively meaningful and valuable form of existence'. Thus in
the stronger sense the 'right to life' involves the right to
lead a meaningful existence and thus to the conditions
necessary for one to lead such an existence. The phrase
'conditions necessary' is not intended to identify a neatly
distinct and possibly independent right, but rather to point
up the evident fact that if a person is to achieve that to
which he has a right, then that may partly depend upon
conditions which it is not in his own power to control or
bring about.

Thus with regard to absolute poverty, one of the features
which makes it absolute is the fact that the conditions
necessary for the absolute poor to escape such an existence
are largely beyond their control to create, at least without
the assistance of outside bodies, such as government schemes

24

or Aid programmes. It is true and important that poor people can 'help themselves', but it often needs the input from the outside of factors which help them to help themselves. It certainly needs the *absence* of factors which work against the poor helping themselves to improve their lot, like high rents or low wages. At another level one can note that the right to freedoms and liberties, such as freedom of speech or liberty of religious expression, also requires the existence of background conditions which are not, except marginally perhaps, in the control of the holder of the right. For the exercise of such rights needs to be protected by the general and known respect by others of that right, backed if necessary by the effective sanction of law.

It is fairly obvious how one can use this basic thesis concerning the right to a qualitatively acceptable life, in order to generate an obligation to help alleviate world poverty. For to say that the right to life involves the right to the conditions necessary for a decent life is to imply that corresponding to this right are duties or obligations on the part of other people to do what they can to promote those conditions. 'Other people' means those people who have it in their power, without putting at risk or destroying the quality of their own lives by so doing, to act in such ways as to create such conditions. Now it is clear that amongst the various agents capable of creating those conditions there must be included most better-off people in Western countries. So the argument runs that most people in the West have a substantial obligation to create the conditions in which extreme poverty can be escaped.

This argument, subject to certain qualifications, is broadly right. It might be thought that it contains the same problem which we met earlier, namely that it would have the consequence that one had a constant duty to do all one could to create those conditions. An incautious statement of it might give that impression, but what follows should show that we have a substantial but not omnipresent duty to do so.

Rights: Some Distinctions

There is little doubt that the topic of 'rights' is one of the most confusing and complex topics in moral and political philosophy, and the following remarks hardly begin to do justice to it: they merely help to indicate the central

25

contention. First of all we should note the use of the word 'right' when it is used to indicate some established or instituted *entitlement,* which exists within the framework of some set of established or instituted rules or laws or established conventions of a social group. It may be an entitlement to receive some benefit or service or an entitlement to some liberty or area of choice. But in either case, there correspond to it established correlative duties on the part of others - officials or people in general - to respect or uphold the right in question. Such rights may be legal rights, constituted by the laws of a particular state, social rights embedded in a particular society's or sub-culture's conventions, they may be the rights of members of an association, or, in an analogous area, the rights of players according to the rules of a game. The general point is that it is primarily a *factual* issue whether or not certain rights do or do not exist. Thus in one country there may be the right to strike or the right to a minimum wage, in another country not. Or in one society husbands have certain socially established rights over their wives, in another not.

Such rights need to be distinguished from the kind of rights which we are after. What we need is some kind of *moral* basis for our argument, a basis which has universal validity or application.[1] Such universal moral rights, if they exist, are quite distinct from legally or conventually established rights, the existence of which varies from place to place. To be sure, there may be good moral reasons for establishing such rights (and in some cases for disestablishing them, as in the case of husbands' rights over wives). However what we are looking for here is a basis for our moral argument not an application of it.

The distinction can be illustrated if we note that when, as in the U.N. Declaration on Human Rights, various 'universal rights' are spelled out - many of them concerning the various conditions necessary to or appropriate to the attainment of a decent existence - there is a crucial ambiguity which is not always noted. At one level the Declaration, and the Covenants which give it fuller legalistic embodiment, attempt to *establish* certain rights as universally binding on all member states. Thus through the gradual process of ratifications and the development of international law, these rights can come to be regarded as internationally established or instituted. It is of course clear that this process is nowhere near complete, since regrettably it just is not the case that the universal rights and obligations established in international law are regarded as having the same degree of legalistic reality as those in national or 'municipal' law.

However the supposition that a given right does become internationally instituted does not automatically entail that, from a moral point of view, such a right ought to have been instituted (any more than that the rights of husbands over wives ought to exist in the societies in which they do exist). Still the move towards the legal establishment of universal rights i.e. of rights universally acknowledged by all countries, is generally paralleled by the view of those who support their establishment that these rights do as a matter of fact reflect a moral basis, and more specifically reflect the idea that there are *in the nature of the case* certain basic rights which all human beings do *universally* share.[2] And this idea points to the second level at which such things as the U.N. Declaration of Human Rights are generally understood: namely as expressing a universal moral affirmation, that all men do *have* certain rights, whether or not the laws or institutions of countries do establish them, and whether or not the international community has progressed towards their emodiment in international convenants.

What then is meant by saying that the proposition that all human beings have certain rights is a moral affirmation? Is it simply a way of saying that there *ought to be established* in various national legal systems, and backed by appropriate international legal institutions, the relevant legal rights? That is to say, to talk of moral rights or universal rights is just an indirect way of talking of legal rights which *ought* to exist (and generally do not exist, at least in any adequate form). Now there is little doubt that when people talk of moral/human/universal rights, they often have no more than this in mind - powerful and effective as this idea of human rights may prove to be in practical terms. What however is philosophically significant about this approach is that it analyses 'moral' rights out into two other more basic notions: the notion of a legal or instituted right and

27

the notion of a moral obligation to promote or maintain that
institutional right. So the morally basic idea is that of
duty or obligation, and the idea of rights derivative. One
moral theory, but by no means the only one, which adopts
this approach is Utilitarianism, for the establishment or
maintenance of institutional rights derive their justification from the primary principle of maximising good in whatever ways are appropriate.

However there is more to the idea of moral rights than is
suggested by the preceding account, and this can be
developed in two quite distinct, though complementary, ways.
The first way of developing the idea of moral rights is to
argue that there is something intrinsic to the nature of a
human being and of human well-being which simply generates
certain requirements for action on the part of fellow human
beings. The second way is to argue, within the Contractarian
tradition of moral and political philosophy, that certain
basic rights form a crucial part of the institutions of
justice which constitute an agreed scheme of co-operation in
a society. This line of thought will be pursued in the next
chapter.

Can these two lines of thought both be accepted? Many
philosophers would regard them as alternative hypotheses or
as forming parts of two rival and mutually incompatible
types of moral theory. Certainly, in the one an agent's
moral commitments are seen as radiating out from him simply
in virtue of his *capacities* to promote the good of human
beings: in the other a man's commitment stems from his being
seen as *playing his part* in a scheme of social co-operation.
Though it is beyond the scope of this book to argue the case
properly, it is possible to argue that a capacity to understand moral relations in *both ways* is intelligible and
common, and a mark of a correct understanding of what
morality is all about. If that makes the moral life a
complicated business, then so be it. It *is* a complicated
business.[3] To be sure the first approach, to which we are
all in thought if not in practice susceptible, is the more
idealistic of the two and asks more of us, whilst the second
approach makes less extensive demands on us, even though
those demands are felt to be more pressing because other
people expect us to play our part. However, in terms of the
theme of this book, the reader need only be convinced of

either of the two approaches, since both independently point
to the same general conclusion.

Human Good

The first approach to rights to be discussed relates to the
traditional Natural Rights doctrine, but it is by no means
intended to be an exposition of that doctrine.[4] Basically
the idea is that we start off with the notion of a human
being as having a particular nature. The proper development
and realisation of that nature constitutes human good, well-
being or fulfilment (or what might be termed 'happiness',
except that happiness tends to be associated too much with
pleasure or getting what you want, to match the richer
notion intended). We may then say that as a natural
corollary to this each human being has a *right* to the
development and realisation of his or her good. That is,
each person's good is something *to-be-promoted*; it is better
that each person's good should be promoted than not promoted;
each person's good ought to be promoted, other things being
equal, by the activities of all those, the agent included,
who are in a position to do so. One may say further, in the
language of justice, that to each person is *due* or owing the
realisation of his or her good.

This is not a statement of a legalistic requirement or
demand. Indeed it is almost its antithesis. It simply
indicates that from a certain objective point of view, each
man's good is of value and ought, in principle, to be
promoted. It does not imply that as moral agents we have a
constant duty to promote the good of others nor does it imply
that in practice one ought to be constantly concerning oneself with the welfare of others. Rather it provides a
perspective from which to view our relations to other human
beings, in that one recognises the propriety of promoting
the good of other human beings, because it is something of
value to be promoted. In other words, talk of rights in
this context involves two claims:
(i) There is something which constitutes human 'good' or
fulfilment;
(ii) It is objectively valuable in whom soever it is, or may
be, placed.
Though the language may seem rather colourless, it is a way
of expressing, at least in part, the idea in Christian
thought - and in that of other religions - that all human

beings are brothers or equal in the sight of God, and the idea more specifically in the Quaker saying that there is 'that of God' in every man. These ideas are given powerful expression in religious language and belief, but are capable of being grasped and accepted on independent grounds.

The claim that any man's good is in principle something to be promoted is very general and vague, and it by no means follows from this that we have an extensive obligation to help alleviate world poverty. For it is quite clear that from the point of view of any one person, there is very little he or she can do to affect the good of more than a few of the many millions on this planet. And someone may feel that *his* response to the principle requires him to promote his own good, - after all he is uniquely placed to do that - the good of his family and friends which by virtue of his close relations he is well placed to promote, and occasionally the good of others in need in his own country or community whom, in cost-effective terms, he can benefit more clearly than those distant overseas. He may also claim that his ongoing respect for the basic rules of morality and for established rights derives partly from the view that such moral practices promote the good of people generally.

Now all these applications of the principle are certainly in order, taken one by one. But the crucial question arises concerning what may be called the *scheduling* of moral priorities, i.e. how to get the balance right between the various competing forms of morally desirable action. Of course it is reasonable to look to one's own good or welfare, present and future - but this must not be confused simply with material self-interest or pursuing one's own pleasure as much as possible. Of course, much emphasis in practice must go to concern for family and friends - indeed we anknowledge special ties of obligation in these cases - but not to the exclusion of other concerns. Of course, there are many needy causes in our own society, but this does not mean that it is appropriate to ignore the plight of those in much greater need overseas. Charity may begin at home, but it certainly does not end there. Of course respect for established moral practices - assuming they are not corrupt - is important, but so is the need to improve them, and more significantly, extend their practical influence further into the international sphere.

There are nevertheless no precise moral formulae or rules for getting the 'balance' right. Much depends in any case on a person's circumstances, his abilities and the particular choices he makes for his commitment - a point developed in Chapter 10. Nevertheless it is one of the recurrent themes of this book that if one's basic attitude is right, then the right sorts of action will generally flow from them. However there are further general considerations which do help to show why, at least within the proper balance for most people (who are better off in Western countries), it should be an important part of one's moral responses to be concerned with world poverty.

(i) It is important to make a distinction between what may crudely be called the *elements* of human good or flourishing and the *conditions* necessary for the continued existence of human good.[5] By the elements of good I mean the various things which collectively constitute what makes human life valuable and worth living. Such things are friendships, loving family relationships, caring for others, creative and productive activities, the exercise of reason, spontaneous enjoyments, recreation and relaxation, sense of community, aesthetic experience and so on. The list is not intended to be exhaustive, but to give an idea of what is meant. Nor is it implied that all of these elements must feature in any one individual's life, though there must at least be some of these.

On the other hand, it is clear that there are various conditions which must exist in order that the elements of a good life can exist. At the limiting end there must of course be the continuing of life, and all that that implies by way of the necessities of life - adequate food, shelter, clothing, etc. But if one is talking of conditions necessary for not merely life but a good life, one is talking of a much greater provision of basic necessities and of a wider range of background conditions necessary for a worthwhile life, such as proper educational facilities, proper health care, social order, general availability of remunerative work and so on.

Now these distinctions provide the context for the following claim. Other things being equal, it is better to help create the conditions necessary for life, i.e. help provide the basic necessities of life, than to be concerned with contributing, either directly or indirectly, to positive good. In a sense of course other things are never equal, since other considerations relevant to the balance always operate - such as variables like one's closeness to others, one's capacity to help and the cost-effectiveness of what one may do. It is *not* of course being suggested that one should never promote the good of one's son, or never for instance work for the maintenance of civil liberties, cheap adult education programmes or other conditions which are necessary for general human flourishing, but instead *only* work for the alleviation of absolute poverty. Far from it. If however one acknowledges the greater importance *in itself* of basic conditions being provided, then that should weigh the balance in the direction of *some* significant commitment to the Third World.

No formal proof can be given for claiming that greater weight morally attaches to the provision of the basic conditions for human life. The priority should strike most people as self-evident once it is spelled out. Perhaps however one can defend the idea to some extent by pointing out that the further a man's condition is away from the ideal of human flourishing, the worse his condition and therefore the more important improvement becomes.

It must however be emphasised that one's special relationships with a few other people such as friends, family, work fellows or neighbours are important. This is not just because of one's proximity and hence much greater capacity to influence their lives. It is also because an important, if often under-recognised, *element* in human flourishing is precisely personal relationships and the subjective valuing of one another which lies at the heart of such face-to-face relations. To contribute to another's good in this way is certainly important, particularly when a person may to lack such a dimension in his or her life, or where one knows that one is one of the few people through whom such relationships are possible for that person.

Nevertheless, that sort of thing can only be part of the story. Moral responsibility does not end with personal relationships. *Personal* caring is a crucial element in moral maturity, provided it is in right proportion: too much of it is a sign of moral onesideness. Wider caring for others, whether in one's own country or overseas, is a quite different kind of caring, but it is equally important. (Someone, for instance, who argued that he was not giving a single penny to any wider cause until he had seen to it that his son was perfectly self-fulfilled, would show severely distorted value priorities, and no doubt misguided parental love as well!) Now one's responsibility towards others in general is in one sense spread thinly over vast numbers of people and is shared with many others. Nevertheless it is real enough. If the idea of one's responsibility being shared by many others seems to dilute one's own responsibility, then the recognition of the extent of the problem should strengthen it again. Consider an analogy: one might think that sharing a cash prize with a 100 million other people would mean one would really get *nothing*, until one realised that the cash prize was worth £800 million. Incidentally the analogy can be applied directly to the present issue: for if the 100 million most affluent people in the west gave let us say ten times this £8 sum to appropriate development schemes, the situation of the poorest 800 million would be transformed.

(ii) The second general consideration relevant to getting the balance right concerns the place of concern for one's own good and how one is to understand this notion. For whilst recognition has been given to the importance of tending to one's own good and of allowing a degree of 'moral free space', it is also important to recognise the limits to this, and also that most of us do in practice exceed these limits in the pursuit of self-interest. It is however the excessive pursuit of one's own good, not the pursuit of it as such, which merits the labels of selfishness or egoism. For *within limits* we each have a 'right' to pursue our own good. Two points may be mentioned which may help to prevent one from setting the limits too far in one's own favour.

(a) The account of human good or fulfilment outlined earlier avoided identifying one's interests with such things as (1) maximising one's own pleasure or the satisfaction of one's desires, (2) maximising the accumulation of material possessions, (3) making or saving money for its own sake or for the sake of (1) and (2), or some combination of these. If a person really identifies his good or interests *in these terms,* then there is indeed little chance that he will do much for the sake of others generally, let alone for the poor of the Third World - except perhaps for some occasional charitable acts done out of embarrassment or the twinges of an annoying conscience. For it is rare that human beings will sustain policies of action which they perceive to be inconsistent with what they identify as their real interests

On the other hand, if someone can come to see that such life policies are either not necessary to a qualitatively valuable life or liable to get in the way of such a life, then he would see the propriety of acting more for the sake of others. Enjoyment is a good thing, but too ruthless a pursuit of it may damage the genuineness of personal relations. Making and saving money and gaining possessions are certainly legitimate and necessary features of typical human existence, but preoccupation with them displaces other values and priorities, and may make anxiety over financial security for instance a negative emotion that colours and distorts one's quality of living.

(b) These points, which will be developed in later chapters do not just support the contention that, to a much greater extent than generally realised, acting for the sake of other is perfectly consistent with the pursuit of one's good, as properly understood. They point to the further factor, stressed by Eric Fromm and others, that one of the chief *sources* of self-fulfilment lies precisely in loving others and acting for the sake of others. [6]

The last few paragraphs have provided a basis for describing how the broad moral principle of promoting the good of human beings in general might yield significant commitments on the part of most people in the West. It is admittedly cast in vague terms. But this just seems to be in the nature of the case, and later chapters will explore further the complexities and variations involved in the commitments of individuals.

It is worth observing that if, having acknowledged this principle, someone still remains unconvinced that he should be concerned about the Third World, then there may have entered into his thinking certain kinds of bias. There may be, that is, an implicit underweighting of the value of certain human beings - for instance, because they are not British (nationalist bias), or not European (ethnic bias), or not Christian (religious bias) or not White (racial bias) etc. For such forms of bias are precluded by the principle itself.

Political, Civil, Economic and Social Rights

If we ask ourselves how in practical terms the *moral* right
to a reasonable life can be implemented as widely as
possible, there is little doubt that, apart from the
concerted efforts of individuals and governments to pursue
development goals in a variety of other ways, the establishment of *institutional rights* which reflect this moral basis
is an important priority. For it is when rights are
institutionalised that there is a greater likelihood of
their being implemented. This involves a two-tier process.
At one level the development of a framework of international
law, through the UN Charter and subsequent detailed
Covenants, puts pressure on governments to render themselves
accountable before world opinion if not international courts.
At another level the effective embodiment of these rights
within the 'municipal' laws of each nation puts pressure on
officials and citizens to play their part in implementing
them.

Commonly a distinction is drawn between political and civil
rights and economic cultural and social rights - indeed there
are two separate U.N. Covenants dealing with these two
groups of rights.[7] Rights in the former group includes
such things as political liberty, freedom of speech,
religious liberty, freedom from assault, freedom from
arbitrary arrest. The latter deal with such things as the
right to the necessities of life such as adequate housing and
adequate food, the right to work, the right to health care,
the right to basic education. The difference between the
two groups can be illustrated by the over-simple generalisation that the former are rights to be free from interfer-
ences of various kinds, the latter rights *to* the provision
of various kinds of thing. Yet the differences must not be
allowed to conceal the deep interconnections between the
two groups: political freedom or freedom from arbitrary
arrest may provide the best context in which the poor can
realise their economic rights. It is certainly important
to challenge the common view that political and civil rights
may be disregarded or suppressed if there is a great need to
promote economic rights. As Evan Luard has remarked,

> Both sets of rights are of the highest importance. But
> they are in no way in conflict with each other. Develop-
> ment is not impeded in a society which respects human
> rights. On the contrary, what evidence we have shows that

that it is assisted.[8]

The argument of this chapter has provided *part* of the basis for claiming that all these institutional rights ought to be established. Conditions such as political freedom, religious freedom and freedom from arbitrary arrest are as essential to the 'good life' as the freedom from hunger and disease. The 'moral right to life' provides a central and unifying justification for the establishment of the whole range of these rights.

Nevertheless the appeal to the right to life does underline the importance of economic rights and show that the realisation of economic rights turns out to be particularly imperative. Reasons for this have been given already. But it is worth adding the point here that the other kinds of rights or liberties are of little value if you lack the effective means to exercise them.[9] If you are starving and want enough to eat, not much else matters.

Emphasis on economic rights is important for a purely pragmatic reason. For it provides a corrective to a common prejudice amongst Western thinkers that human rights just are political and civil rights. If we are in earnest about human rights, we must be as much in earnest about the right to a reasonable standard of living as about political rights. The temptation to be selective is understandable. After all if in other parts of the world political freedom or the right not to be killed, tortured or arbitrarily imprisoned is abused, such abuses are not of *our* doing. The situation however is rather different when we turn to economic rights. For on their realisation we do have an influence, both through our economic practices and through our tendency towards indifference. As John Madeley, says, reporting the remark of an African Diplomat, "Human rights begin with breakfast".[10]

Chapter 4

SOCIAL JUSTICE

Charity

The idea of a right to life has been defended and developed, and it has been applied to the context of world poverty to yield a significant obligation to assist. This argument already employs, albeit implicitly and at a very simple level, a concept of *justice*. For if someone has a right to something, then that thing is *due* to him and from others. The concept of justice however is a complex one, and if it is developed can give further support to the basic argument. It is worth asking first why an appeal to justice is often made by those concerned with world development. For apart from the intrinsic merits of an appeal to justice, there is an important pragmatic motive for doing so.

One reason undoubtedly for appealing to justice is to counteract the tendency for people to think of their response to world poverty in terms of charity, benevolence or kindness, or to be more precise, in terms of "It is simply a matter of charity". The implication of this way of talking is usually that acts of charity or kindness are *not* requirements of morality or duties. They are either simply natural feelings or expressions of a personal ideal. The claim that it *is* a matter of moral obligation to respond to world poverty is often couched in terms of justice as a reaction to this, and whilst the slogan 'Justice not Charity' oversimplifies the issue, it helps to make a substantive point. What then is wrong with the 'charity' approach?

A possible misunderstanding must be removed first. The argument is *not* directed against the motives of kindness, compassion, charity, love, agape - or whatever is one's preferred term for this positive and dynamic psychological attitude. For at the end of the day, it is this, in its richest and fullest form, which provides the motivational dynamics behind any wholehearted commitment to combat world poverty - or any other major social ills, in the world or nearer to home. In a sense this book is directed precisely towards those who do feel kindness or concern and who acknowledge that this is grounded in a moral ideal or a moral obligation: these reflections may strengthen that concern and clarify the moral insights upon which it is based, by drawing out the deeper implications of what 'caring for others' involves. The criticisms which follow are directed mainly at what may be called a pre-moral or non-moralized version of charity or benevolence, a version which is implied by the fact that helping the poor is seen as 'merely' or 'simply' a matter of benevolence or charity.

For the force of the 'merely' is generally this: though we have reason to help the poor, to the extent that we are activated by relevant feelings of benevolence and ackowledge these feelings to be important to us, moral reasons do not come into it. Thus, coupled with his benevolent concerns, someone may either just not have thought about the moral issues, or, having thought about them, he may reject the idea that he or others have any moral obligation to help the poor.

Now it might be thought that such an approach was on the right lines. After all a person could be *very* generous in outlook and might indeed do as much as, if not more than, someone else who thought he had a duty to do so. Nevertheless it must be said that there are many limitations to such an outlook and that it is vitally important that the moral arguments are understood and acknowledged.

(a) Though it is possible for someone to be very benevolent but not acknowledge any duty, nevertheless the tendency is for moral considerations to be more powerful. Without them the tendency is for someone to put money in a collecting tin, give jumble to a good cause, occasionally write a £5 cheque for an emergency appeal, but do no more. Relevant and appropriate as such gestures are, they are hardly enough. It seems reasonable to suppose that a firm understanding of the moral propriety of such actions will make people more generous in these ways and also induce them to do other kinds of things as well.

(b) A further limitation is that if *my* concern is purely humanitarian, I have no ground for recommending that *others* should help. All I can do is to say how nice it is to feel benevolence and hope that others will feel likewise. What I cannot do is to tell others that they *ought* to be or feel generous. In particular, I cannot tell government or public bodies that they ought to be generous or to give Aid or more Aid. For on the non-moral basis I have adopted I can do no more than *hope* that Government Ministers feel benevolent or reflect the benevolence of the Electorate. Even 'hope' is a little odd here since the natural reason for the hope is that they will do what is decent or what they ought - and that evaluation is a moral one and not allowed on the view being considered.

(c)   The oddity of the view just imagined concerning Aid brings out a crucial point. Though it is tempting to think of Government Aid as parallel to private acts of charity, as something 'beyond the requirements of duty', it would be extraordinary to suppose that Aid-giving was something for which moral reasoning was irrelevant! Politicians may argue about levels of Aid and the *relative* weight of different goals for public spending, but it is hard to see what sense could be made of the idea that there was nothing to be said, morally speaking, for giving Aid.

(d)   In fact there is much to be said for giving Aid, and the complexity of the reasons for this, discussed elsewhere, shows quite clearly the inadequacy of the 'merely charity' approach. For the person who concentrates on charity makes two related assumptions. (i) Helping the poor consists (at least primarily) in *giving*, donating, collecting and transferring money (or maybe food, clothing) abroad. (ii) Since helping the poor is something over and above the demands of morality, it is an activity which does not affect or call into question the basic structures of society, international institutions and so on. For if it did this, one would have to use moral arguments in order to question the legitmacy of those structures and institutions.

As soon as one realises that many of the ways of helping solve world poverty involve changing institutions and practices, for instance in international trading activities, one realises that complex moral arguments are needed to justify those changes. It is this idea which lies behind the slogans of people advocating development such as 'Justice not Charity' and 'Trade not Aid'. These slogans oversimplify matters, since charity as such is not displaced by considerations of justice, nor is Aid to be dismissed if the emphasis is put on equitable trade practices. But the two slogans do at least make the twin points that what we do for developing countries is a requirement of justice and hence morality, and that what is at stake is our whole economic relationship with poorer countries, not some separate act of giving conducted in isolation from everything else we do.

(e) One can approach the last basic point from a different angle, if one focusses on another weakness of the 'merely charity' outlook. For there is a tendency in this approach to think of what one is responding to in rather limited terms. It is of course profoundly important that what one responds to is the *suffering* and misfortune of human beings. But if one's response is limited to that, one has not thought out the tragedy of poverty very far. In any case, apart from extreme cases of natural disasters like an earthquake where it may seem that "It cannot be helped", most people - even those who think in terms of 'charity only' - actually find themselves passing judgments such as "Poverty like that ought not to exist" or "They ought not to allow it to exist". Now this 'ought' shows that they are at least implicitly thinking in moral terms, in terms of responsibility and of human decisions which could be different.

The conclusion to this is that in responding to poverty, one is not just responding to suffering as such, one is responding to suffering that ought not to exist, to a failure to secure basic rights, to the inadequacies of human institutions which generate the suffering. No one who sees these implications would wish to see helping as 'mere charity', disconnected from moral considerations, for one's humanitarian feelings engage with the problem on a moral level.

Two Arguments

How then can appeals to justice strengthen the moral arguments for helping to alleviate world poverty? Appeals to justice can be made at two levels, the first more controversial than the second. The first centres on the idea of exploitation, the second on the idea of basic needs.

Consider first the basic economic relationships between rich and poor countries. It is very plausible to argue that in many respects the relationships between Western governments, institutions or business companies and developing countries and their peoples have been in varying degrees exploitative in character. That is, the relationships have been determined by the stronger party to the detriment of the weaker party in such a way as to offend against canons of justice in economic dealings. Thus richer nations determine the terms

of trade to their advantage, i.e. how much they pay for
primary commodities and how much they receive for their
manufactured goods. Or transnational companies may fix wage
levels for workers in poor countries at very low levels.

What makes such transactions exploitative or unjust can be
caught in the intuitive idea: would the stronger party be
happy with a transaction if he had been in the weaker
party's shoes? Now whilst it is neither helpful nor correct
to take the view of exploitation favoured by Marxists and to
say that all Capitalist transactions are inherently
exploitative, it does seem that a candid appraisal of the
West's relations with developing countries leaves much to be
desired on this count. Thus on such an account of justice
as fairness in economic transactions it is possible both to
criticise the past record and to recommend reforms in such
practices from now on.

Powerful as this line of criticism is, there is a more
significant argument to hand which, being less 'politically'
controversial in character, is more likely to gain general
support. What perhaps gives the edge to the argument
concerning exploitation is the fact that the *results* of
exploitation are that people live degrading lives in absolute
poverty: exploitation is bad enough anyway, but it is this
consequence which is particularly disturbing. For there is
surely something *inherently unjust* that people should live
in such poverty. Now if there is an inherent injustice in
people living in absolute poverty, then it is important to
note that there may be many causes of such poverty, or more
relevantly many removable causes. It is not just exploitation as described above which causes poverty. It may be
government policies and bureaucratic inefficiencies within
developing countries which partly cause poverty, or let it
continue to exist when it could be reduced. One can argue
that the inadequencies of Western Aid policies cause poverty
in the sense that bigger and better Aid policies would further
reduce poverty. Protectimist policies in the West against
Third World imports cause or perpetuate some poverty which
would be alleviated if we did not impose quotas and tariffs.
So likewise more generally does Western opposition to the
implementation of the 'New International Economic Order',
and at the most general level one can say that the
indifference of people in the rich North causes some of the
poverty, insofar as less indifference would result in less
poverty.

Now it is possible for people to argue: "So what? What is wrong with protectionism if it is in our interests, or our opposition to the NIEO if the NIEO is not in our interests?[1] Why should we be held responsible for what we would have prevented if we had actively intervened?" And no doubt it will be objected, since in practical contexts the word 'cause' is a partly evaluative term and is used to mean 'a factor relevant to bringing about or sustaining an evil which *ought not to exist*', that it prejudges the issue to talk of these factors as *causes* of poverty.

The last point may be accepted since it is precisely the identification of factors which ought not to exist that we are after. But the reason why they ought not to exist is because there is something unjust, not something merely to be regretted, about the existence of extreme poverty. Or more exactly, its existence is unjust insofar as it is in human power to reduce it, consistent with other morally relevant considerations. It is precisely because extreme poverty is partly linked to our deliberate policies, in as much as different policies would result in rather less of such poverty, that we have an obligation to alter those policies - provided, that is, that overall other moral considerations are taken properly into account.

Basic Needs

What then are the grounds for claiming that it is a matter of social justice that people be helped to escape from extreme poverty?[2] Let us start with a premiss which would be accepted by a wide range of people in a country such as Britain. This premiss is that people *ought* to be protected from extreme poverty, and if they do fall into some form of extreme hardship then they ought to be helped out of it. In some sense a society has a responsibility to realise these goals, and if it does not do so, where it has the capacity to do so, then it can hardly claim to be a civilised society. Now when we talk of a society's responsibilities we mean - or we ought to mean - at least two things. First, individuals, who collectively make up that society, ought to act in certai ways, and second, organs of government and administration, which act in the name of that society, ought to pursue policies of a certain sort. Thus people are protected or rescued from extreme hardship or calamity partly through the efforts of individuals who, as individuals or through private organisations, do what they can to help, and partly through the pursuit of these social goals through various mechanisms of the 'welfare state'. Not only are such things as free health services, unemployment and sickness benefits and pension schemes relevant, but also, more positively, social and economic policies designed to create full employment or a not too unequal distribution of wealth and pay.

Those politically to the Right will, if they are committed to this goal, emphasise the role of private individuals and organisations in this process, and will also tend to think of the moral basis in terms of charity and benevolence. Those politically to the Left will emphasise the role of the State and its bureaucratic agents in pursuing this objective, and will tend to think of the protection from hardship in terms of social justice. Nevertheless most politically aware people would recognise that *some* mixture of the two kinds of activity is required and that a society which has the ability to do so ought to pursue this policy of, in a sense, guaranteeing a kind of social and economic minimum or safety net. That some people slip through the net is probably inevitable. However what we are talking about is what ought to happen and about a rationale for this.

Upon this basis the following pragmatic argument can proceed. For *if* the reader is one who is prepared to accept the force of the above argument, then he ought to be open to its application in the international sphere. That is, if it really is a requirement of morality that within a society extreme poverty ought to be alleviated so far as is possible, then surely it is a requirement of morality for this to be done within the global society or international community. To be sure, it is easier said than done. The reality of international society or community is not as *well* established as that of national societies or states. Yet it is clearly established to some degree, so there ought to be recognised some degree of obligation anyway. Barbara Ward put the approach very well when she wrote:

> ...We can see aid to development and the evolution of a sane world monetary and development policy as simple applications at the right level of policy which we entirely accept inside our own domestic communities. Aid is a sort of world tax which should go to basic social world needs - in diet, health, family planning, in schooling and

43

housing. We take such policies for granted at home. But the planet is our home and we must learn to take comparable policies for granted there.[3]

Opposition to the argument will, of course, come from those who assume or argue that in international affairs there exist no such corresponding claims of social justice (even if it is granted, which it may not be, that such claims exist within societies). That is, it will be objected that such claims of justice cannot be made by either nation states or groups of people within states upon either other nation states or groups of people within other states. This objection will stem either from a political doctrine within the theory of international relations to the effect that sovereign states have an absolute right to pursue their own interests, or from a moral doctrine, such as cultural relativism, which limits effective obligation to members of one's own society.

These two forms of opposition to the international dimension to ethics will reappear elsewhere in this book.[4] Here it is appropriate to develop the main argument concerning *social justice*, whether in the national or international sphere. Whilst acceptance of the preceding approach by no means belongs exclusively to the thinking of those of the political Left, it *is* clear that the requirement that extreme poverty be alleviated is a requirement of justice not charity or benevolence, and that an important element in achieving this must lie in the public policies of governments. However much it may be the case that charity ideally or in its fulles Christian form includes a concern for justice and is power- ful in its influence, in practice appeal to charity or benevolence is not treated as a demand but as an optional extra and is not very effective in getting sustained action.

But a second reason for preferring to think of the allevi- ation of poverty in terms of justice is that this claim can be built into a wider conception of justice or of what constitutes a just society. It is not for instance just extreme poverty which a society has a duty to alleviate or prevent, but various kinds and degrees of condition which prevent people from leading satisfactory lives. If it were, incidentally, just extreme poverty, then by any reasonable definition of extreme poverty, very few people in Britain would qualify for protection - though the relative and real poverty of many is in fact very much a matter for social concern.

The preceding account of social justice relies partly on the idea of a *minimum* below which people are not meant to fall. This may raise the query: isn't the notion of a 'minimum' terribly relative and fluid? Since this query is often a preliminary move in an argument against doing anything, it is worth making the following comments. If indeed the only requirement of justice here were the alleviation of extreme poverty and nothing more, then there might be problems about where to draw the line, how much - i.e. how little - allevi- ation is required and so on, when one is considering the poor within Western countries. On the other hand there could be no quibbling about which side of the line the 800 million absolute poor fall.

But if one sees the requirement of social justice as not just concerned with the extreme but with the range of conditions which in varying degrees mar people's lives, then the objection concerning the relativity of terms loses its grip. One can still insist that the greater the hardship or the worse the poverty, the more pressing the need for social action. But it is 'more pressing', not 'exclusively important'. For, within the resources available, there are other things connected with making worthwhile lives more possible which are also important. Much of the justification, for instance, for the public provision of education, parks and playgrounds, recreational facilities and so on, surely lies in the fact that this helps enable people to live well, not just to live.

Rawls' Theory

These ideas may seem intuitively acceptable and therefore in need of no further support. However it is useful to tie them into a wider conception of justice. This can be done in two ways. First one can link the idea of a society's obligation to protect people from poverty or hardship to the discussion of the preceding chapter. If the right to a reasonable life expresses a significantly pressing moral claim on society to maintain the conditions necessary for a reasonable life, then the right to life forms the basis of the requirements of social justice.

But there is no doubt that the idea of social justice can be

45

given powerful extra support if we consider the 'contractarian' approach to the justification of moral principles. This is the approach taken in a recent and influential book by John Rawls entitled *A Theory of Justice*.[5] Rawls sees the principles of social justice as the fundamental principles governing the basic institutions, rules and rights of a society. What is valuable about the book is that it presents a distinctive rationale for accepting principles of justice and also a distinctive set of principles. Both the rationale and the principles constitute a clear and attractive articulation of what may be called the liberal democratic approach to justice.

Rawls' method for formulating principles of justice belongs to the ideal contract tradition in political theory, and is intended to represent a system of justice as one that would be agreed upon by free and equal rational agents. Rawls argues that principles of justice are those principles which would be chosen by parties placed in a certain hypothetical situation, which he calls the 'original position'. In this position each person is a rational self-interested agent who wants to choose principles which are to govern the society in which he is to live. *But* - and this is the dramatic qualification - each person is behind what Rawls calls the 'veil of ignorance', in that he knows nothing of his personal circumstances. He knows nothing about whether he is rich or poor, or whether he is intelligent and endowed with abilities or not, or about what his own conception of the good is i.e. what sort of life he wants to lead. This veil of ignorance guarantees lack of bias, and Rawls claims that under such conditions, parties in the original position would agree on a set of principles, and that these principles constitute the principles of justice which are applicable and acceptable to us real agents who live in real societies in the real world.

What then are the fundamental principles which Rawls argues are the principles of justice because they would be chosen in the original position? To quote Rawls:

First: each person is to have an equal right to the most extensive basic liberty compatible with a similar liberty for others.

Second: social and economic inequalities are to be arranged so that they are both (a) reasonably expected to be to everyone's advantage, and (b) attached to positions and offices open to all.[6]

According to Rawls (1) has lexical priority over (2) in the sense that, at least in a society in a reasonable state of economic development, it must be fully implemented before the second principle is implemented. Of the two principles in (2), it is (2)a which is the more significant. It is called the 'difference principle' and amounts to the idea that the only justified differences in wealth and economic status are those which result in those who are poorest being better off than they would be were society otherwise organised. Rawls assumes, no doubt rightly, that given certain facts about economic incentives, some inequalities are necessary in order for an economy to work efficiently and thus to benefit everyone in it, for instance through the use of taxed surplus wealth to finance welfare provisions. Rawls claims that the Difference Principle would be chosen in the Original Position because the parties would want, in their state of ignorance, to pursue a 'maximin' policy, that is the policy in which the worst outcome for oneself would be better than the worst outcome of any other policy.

To subject these ideas to detailed criticism would not be appropriate in this book. Rawls' basic approach gives some insight into the idea of morality as a set of principles for a society agreed upon by people for mutual benefit. The veil or ignorance condition captures, in a graphic way, the idea that these principles already reflect a moral point of view in which all people are given equal weight. One would get a *very* different picture of morality, and of justice as a central part of morality, if one thought of the principles of morality or justice as somehow settled beyond criticism by the *actual* agreements of fully informed rational agents pursuing their own individual or group interests, or by the semi-conscious process of social and cultural pressures creating moral codes which are sustained because they do more or less serve most people's interests.

To be sure, the actual codes of morality or justice which exist do tend to reflect the compromises of powerful interests groups or the influences of social custom. To be sure, some philosophers have argued that such conceptions of morality are indeed correct or at least beyond further criticism from a supposed ideal point of view. Yet if one believes that there is something more basic and unchanging about principles of morality or justice, one must look beyond the fluctuating consequences of interest-groups and custom. Rawls' book is an affirmation that such a perennial idea exists. Without it the cause of addressing problems such as poverty or of generally striving to make a better world would be doomed from the start.

There is more doubt however about how right Rawls is about the principles which he advocates, or about the derivation of these principles from the original position. He is clearly right that the establishment and protection of liberties, both political and civil liberties, are vital elements of a just society, as classical liberal thinkers were right to stress. (His insistence on the priority of the principle of equal liberty is however unjustified.) The 'difference principle', on the other hand, gives expression to something less well recognised by traditional liberals and better recognised by socialists, namely that people also have rights to the conditions necessary for a reasonable existence, as well as to liberties, which are meaningless anyway unless one has adequate means to exercise them.

Yet the 'difference principle' is in some respects one-sided. As we saw earlier, justice requires that it is not merely the *poorest* that are protected but rather a range of people whose life-chances are varyingly curtailed by their social and economic circumstances and who are thus to be considered in the decisions of government and policy-makers. Furthermore if the 'difference principle' could be implemented in such a way that the minimum level of wealth was well above what would be regarded as a reasonable standard of living, it is doubtful if justice would require the satisfaction of the 'difference principle'. It is also doubtful if parties in the original position would prefer the 'difference principle' to the principle of guaranteeing a reasonable minimum level of wellbeing.

Justice then requires amongst other things that certain kinds and degrees of inequality be removed. For instance, people should be protected from certain conditions of poverty: the worse the conditions, the greater the efforts to prevent or remove them. The attempts of people to further their own good should be adequately backed by provision of education, opportunities and so on, and by the absence of negative factors such as class or racial discrimination. These are some of the elements of social justice to which the 'difference principle' roughly points. A full account of justice would include, amongst other things, further elaboration of the place of civil and political liberties, and also of the principles of fairness in economic transactions discussed earlier. It is arguable that Rawls' 'original position' *method* for deriving principles of justice would in fact yield something like these principles rather than his own. But to defend that lies beyond the scope of this book.[7]

Rawls' own discussion incidentally is almost entirely in terms of justice within a nation-state society. But it seems possible to apply the approach to the international sphere and to ask oneself the same kind of question as that implicit in the original position.[8] If I did not know what position I would be in - whether a rich Northerner or a very poor Southerner - and I was considering what principles should govern international society and its economic transactions, would I not come up with certain principles which, if implemented, would *considerably* improved my likely life-chances in a Third World country? The argument does not transfer entirely since international society is relatively less well established. Nevertheless the *force* of the analogy cannot possibly be missed, unless one is completely cynical about international ethics altogether.[9]

One line of argument concerning justice has not yet been mentioned. It goes as follows: It is a requirement of justice that all inequalities, whether within or between countries, in the wealth of individuals be eliminated, and hence social policies designed to correct inequalities should be pursued as effectively as possible. Egalitarianism will in fact be discussed more fully later. But briefly, there does not seem to be anything *inherently* wrong with inequalities of wealth. Nevertheless generally *gross* inequalities of wealth are strongly indicative of various forms of injustice, such as exploitation by the powerful, lack of provision for those in need, economic or political discrimination against minority groups and so on.

The ideal of a society in which all people lead a satisfactory life is not the ideal of a society in which all have the same amount of wealth or material possessions. For that would only be true if the good life consisted precisely in having such things or having as much as one could of them. But it is not. Nevertheless there is much in the practical thrust of egalitarian thinking which is to be respected, provided it stems from a desire to see the poor less poor, and not to see the rich less rich (except as a means to the former goal). Envy is not a good basis for moral thought.

In this and the previous two chapters the philosophical framework for the central proposition of this book has been set out. Most of these ideas will reappear, either assumed or developed, in various contexts throughout the book. We are at any rate now in a position to look more closely at the nature of our obligations in the context of a more detailed picture of our global circumstances.

PART TWO: GLOBAL ISSUES

Chapter 5

THE THIRD WORLD AND THE WEST

The Capacity to Help

In the previous chapters our central proposition has been defended by combining two factual claims with two moral claims. The factual claims are that 800 million people live in absolute poverty and that Western countries are by comparison very affluent indeed. The moral claims are that we ought to promote human good wherever it may be and that we ought to promote social justice.

There is little doubt that if as individuals we are concerned about world poverty, there are effective things which we can do, at least at the level of financial giving. Financial donations to charities whose work is at grass roots level will clearly help with genuine development. And yet no doubt many will feel that there is something missing from the argument that *collectively* we have a substantial obligation. For a substantial obligation entails the existence of a substantial *capacity* to render development assistance. And it may be doubted whether Governments, multinational companies, Trades Unions or people as a whole *do* have the capacity to render assistance which really does help the *poor* of developing countries on a large scale.

This may be partly because it is doubtful whether we have the *will* to do so; that is, whether we have the motivational resources to do so. Governments inevitably, it may be said, promote national interests and most people promote their own interests, whatever a few idealists may do or think. It may also be partly because it may be doubted whether, whatever attempts at aid or development we may make, the overall consequences of our involvement are generally not helpful to genuine development.

This is a challenging line of thought and deserves a reply. The reply will take us into controversial areas of economic, political and historical interpretation. In the following analysis no attempt is made to substantiate all the claims: the reader will have to judge how far it corresponds to his own informed judgments and knowledge of these areas.[1] What is of interest in the present context are the broad moves in

51

a complex debate. Still one general objective is to make good the claim that Western countries do have an *extensive capacity* to alleviate absolute poverty in (at least most) developing countries. If this is so, we are not debarred from claiming that they have an obligation to do so, however short they fall in practice.

When we talk of the capacity to help, what in fact does the concept 'help' mean? It is important to note that the concept of helping someone involves not only (a) positive help i.e. positive action which improves the situation, but also (b) refraining from action which (i) causes a worsening of the situation, and (ii) hinders or prevents that person or others on his behalf from improving the situation.

The assessment of whether one country, for instance, helps another country with development will therefore turn out to be a complex matter. This is partly because the assessment depends on what the intentions of the 'helper' are, and partly because it depends upon what the overall consequences turn out to be, whatever the intentions. It follows from these points about helping that the West's obligation to help is a complex one. It implies that, apart from any active help we give, we should refrain from economic practices which actually cause poverty, and we put no obstacles in the way of the efforts of developing countries to help themselves to improve their situation.

If one asks oneself why it is that the West has an extensive capacity to help, it must surely rest on the fact that we are so deeply involved in the affairs of many developing countries that there are extensive opportunities for assistance. This involvement has many facets - economic, political, cultural, intellectual and ideological.

Imagine by contrast a situation in which we knew of the existence of a country in which there existed appalling poverty, but we had no links with that country. There was no trade, no currency convertibility, no common language and little or no knowledge of each other's language. Here the possibilities for helping are minimal. They are 'minimal' not 'non-existent' since even here there is always the possibility of initiative, of starting to build the connections which would enable more effective help to be given: no doubt missionaries saw themselves as 'putting themselves' into a position to help by literally taking themselves, faith and skills in hand, into the bush. So our imagined situation is not quite like that of a distance planet whose people were in a dire condition but were quite beyond the reach of our help.

Nevertheless the imagined situation is quite unlike that which exists vis-à-vis the relations between many rich and poor countries. For where we have extensive trading connections, there are many things that can be done. Where there is currency convertibility, Aid can be sent. Where there is a common language or commonly known language, there are significant possibilities for assistance from teachers, doctors or technologists.

But the imagined case serves another purpose, one which may have already crossed the reader's mind. For it is somewhat like the actual situation vis-à-vis the relations between the West and countries officially committed to Communist systems of government. Here the reason why a high degree of involvement does not exist is because such countries choose to avoid Western involvement and to exist largely in isolation from Western economic activity. It is significant that in Britain there is a tendency to think of different poor countries as having different degrees of priority or claim on our concern and the allocation of Aid. Thus, broadly, Commonwealth countries, such as India, Pakistan or Bangladesh - three countries in which there also happens to be much of the worst poverty - and various countries in Africa, tend to evoke more of a response than countries in Latin America, for instance. Countries which are sympathetic to Western ideology or economic interests evoke our concern rather more than those with a more Communist ideology.

These broad differentiations, and indeed other more subtle ones, will be based on a number of different reasons, some more respectable than others. Criteria such as importance for our own economic interests, political orientation on the right-left spectrum, usefulness for our strategic interests, no doubt do play an important, and indeed too important, role in determining the contours of relative importance. What is rather more relevant, from a moral point of view, is to recognise the following two points.
(a) Absolute poverty is, in principle, something which the rich ought to be concerned with, wherever it exists. Absolute poverty is equally terrible, whether it is in Kenya,

Argentina, Cuba or China.

(b) What *primarily* ought to govern the relative levels and types of concern is the availability of channels for effective action. If a poor communist country does not receive any or much aid from us, it should not be because the poor in that country do not deserve our concern, it should rather be for the reason that the Government of that country has not developed or deliberately stopped any appropriate channels for helping.

Various examples of the different types of involvement will be mentioned when we consider the full implications of 'helping'. Let us put on one side for the moment that particular form of 'helping' associated with Charity, assistance or Aid. This is the active giving of money or services where the public or explicit intention - whatever the private motive - is that what is given should improve the situation of the receiver of the help. Let us consider rather the broad question: Does Western involvement with developing countries help them with their development, and in particular with the reduction of absolute poverty? This is not primarily a question about intentions, but about the general consequences of our total relationships. This is a crucial issue. For if it turned out that by and large our involvement is not beneficial, then the opportunities which that involvement may provide for active help may be over-shadowed by the bad consequences of the involvement itself. And if that were so, then one would be inclined to agree with Tolstoy when he said that the rich man is prepared to do anything to ease the burden of the poor man... except get off his back.[2]

Credit and Debit

What one has to consider is a kind of balance sheet, in which claims that the West's involvement has benefitted or is benefitting developing countries are set against claims that harm of various kinds is done and that much poverty can be traced causally to the practices of Governments, Companies or people in the West. This is of course already a political exercise. For how one draws up the balance sheet will depend upon what one counts as progress and its reverse, and upon what one counts as the main *causes* of the impediments to progress: for the identification of a 'cause' involves evaluative issues. Still that rough list will without

claims to completeness or justification, provide a
heuristic device for illustrating the complexity of the
issue.

On the one hand, it can be said that the impact of the West
on Developing countries has helped to give them many basic
skills - in medicine, agriculture, finance, bureaucratic
organisation, government, commerce and so on. All of these
are essential for any country today if it is to proceed with
development. Furthermore, Western economic involvement has
been and continues to be essential for Developing countries
to acquire the technology, machines or manufactures which
they need for development through their *exporting* to the
West primary commodities such as minerals, rubber, tobacco
and foodstuffs. Education, medicine and modern agriculture
have all helped to transform the life-chances of people in
developing countries, and have improved the quality of life
for the large number who are not still caught in the poverty
trap.

It is of course true that what gave Developing countries
their existence and geographical identities was the colon-
ising and organising activities of Western nations, who
managed in the process of colonisation largely to supplant
traditional ethnic cultures and traditional conceptions of
the 'quality of life' with Western cultural and economic
values. So it may seem circular - or at least suspect - to
measure the benefits in terms of *our* standards not theirs.
There is an important point here. We should not assume that
Developing countries will want to retain or adopt much of
our Western values - whether of the capitalist or the
communist variety - and not keep or resurrect indigenous
values. But one cannot put the clock back. Any developing
country's development objectives will inevitably be a blend
of assimilated Western values and of other ethnic values.
It remains by and large true that for the vast majority of
Third World leaders and their peoples, the overall impact
of Western practices and values, in commerce, medicine,
education, technology, science, culture and religion, has
been beneficial; that is, beneficial by the standards of
evaluation accepted by them, not just by us.

On the other side of the balance sheet, a wide range of
points can be made. One can point out how in a general way
the overall impact of the West has not been an entire success

story. It is often pointed out that modern medicine has give
rise to the population explosion, because, successful enough
as it has been to increase life-expectancy dramatically, it
has not been successful enough to give ordinary parents the
confidence needed to want to limit families.[3] Western
'individualism' has eroded traditional family and community
values, and also given rise to forms of entrepreneur
capitalism which, without the adequate check from respect for
others' rights, has produced alarming disparities of wealth.
Much tribal antagonism can be attributed to the arbitrary
carve-up of territories in the Colonial past: and so on.
These points certainly bear upon our past involvement and
concern things which in a sense cannot be undone. It is
possible to feel, if one is a Westerner, a certain sense of
guilt about these and other features of our colonial past, and
if that adds strength to one's commitment to development now,
so much the better. But out main concern should be to single
out a number of specific ways in which Western Countries,
chiefly through the agencies of Government and transnational
companies, are *now actively* causing poverty or hindering
progress or failing to take up obvious strategies which
would help. The list is not exhaustive but it does indicate
the *range* of ways in which we might be said to be 'not
helping matters'.

(i) There are certain patterns of commercial activity which
have to be described as 'exploitative' or 'unjust' by common
standards of fair dealing.[4] For example:-
(a) Through their economic power Western Governments or
Companies may dictate the 'terms of trade' to their advantage.
Thus it might be determined how many tractors have to be sold
in order to acquire so many tons of a primary commodity. The
OPEC action in 1973 was of course an example of economic
control exercised against us by another powerful group, and
we did not like it very much.
(b) Multinational companies sometimes pay workers in their
subsidiary companies in developing countries extremely low
wages which scarcely provide subsistence living. The wages
of tea-pickers has come in for adverse criticism in this
respect, but it is only one of many cases.
(c) Multinational companies sometimes engage in the ruthless promotion of their goods in developing countries, where
those goods do harm or divert resources from development
objectives. Examples which come to mind are those of baby

milk powder and high-tar cigarettes.[5]

(ii)   There are certain features of Government Aid policies
and of the Investment policies of large and small companies
which call for criticism, not because they are deliberately
exploitative, but because of their actual effects which are
often unforeseen.   Indeed the Governments of developing
countries are often in favour of these policies.
(a)   Partly as a legacy of the colonial past, developing
countries are often dependent upon one or two export crops
(sugar, tea, coffee, bananas, etc.).   Thus monocultures
develop and large areas of land are used for the production
of the export crop.   The advantage of this is that such
crops can earn useful foreign exchange, but the disadvantages
are that reliance on one or two types of export makes a
country very vulnerable to fluctuations in world market
prices, and that greater diversification would help ride
these fluctuations better and also cater for local food needs
better.
(b)   Both Governments and Companies have a tendency to prefer
capital-intensive projects to labour-intensive projects.
There is a preference for a prestige hospital to a number
of low profile health clinics, a big plastic shoe factory to
the support for traditional leather craft industries,
machinery for agri-business to appropriate technologies for
peasants with small holdings of land.   A sophisticated
factory may increase a Country's G.N.P., but if it puts
people out of work or excludes the poor from progress, it
hardly contributes to genuine development.

(iii)   There are certain areas in which Western governments
are showing a distinct reluctance to acknowledge the
necessity for change.   This reluctance is a contributory
factor amongst the difficulties experienced by Third World
countries in their development efforts.[6]
(a)   The world trading system is becoming highly unstable.
Fluctuating prices, particularly for developing countries
with only one or two major exports, are very damaging
economically, because they prevent effective forward planning.
The West's reluctance to accept the 'New International
Economic Order' can be seen as an obstacle to progress
(including our own progress according to the Brandt Report).
(b)   A major step forward in development for many developing
countries is in the development of their own capacity to

process raw materials before they are exported, and to produce their own manufactures for export. The success of this depends upon sufficient markets in Western countries. However there is a growing tendency for Western Governments to engage in protectionism with tariffs and import quotas. Protectionism is not in itself morally wrong, but the fact that its operation impedes development and hence the alleviation of absolute poverty must count as a moral reason against it. But the main point at issue here is that, whether it is right or wrong, it certainly has bad consequences for world poverty.

(c)   More generally, the capacity to exercise economic control over its own affairs by a developing country and thus to have greater 'autonomy' will ensure greater effectiveness in its development efforts. Therefore efforts or attitudes of Western Governments and Companies which limit such autonomy or constitute interference, are an impediment to autonomy. As a corollary to this, one can point to the relatively small amount of representation which developing countries have on international financial institutions such as the I.M.F. or the World Bank, as the Brandt Commission noted and criticised.[7] More 'say' in the decision making of international bodies for developing countries would certainly help them with their development efforts, and would certainly be more democratic.

(iv)   It must however be added that *some* Governments in developing countries are not themselves wholly committed to combatting their own poverty. This may be through a general unwillingness to take effective measures, or through condoning or tolerating racial or religious oppression of minority groups. Nor are right-wing governments renowned for their respect for human rights, including the right to a decent living. The relevance of this to the present argument about whether the West is helping is of course this. If Western Governments, for reasons of economics, strategy, racial affinity or some other factor of self-interest, condone, support or even supply arms to such a Government, then they are effectively hindering the alleviation of poverty. This would be so at least if there is any real chance that a change in a Western Government's attitude would *either* help to replace such a government with one more sympathetic to the poor, *or* help to soften the attitude of such a government to its own poor.

It will be apparent from the preceding discussion that there is a 'debit' side to our involvement with developing countries. However the reason for dwelling on the different examples at much greater length than the statement of the 'credit' side, has not been to herald the conclusion: "Net balance: we're doing more harm than good". Rather it was to indicate the many different areas where we could and ought to initiate reform, changes of policy and so on. The overall verdict is that developing countries, which are within the 'Western' sphere of influence, do benefit from being involved with Western countries, but that they *could benefit a lot more* if certain changes were made.

To put the matter starkly: If extensive Western Capitalist-oriented economic, technological and financial involvement in the Third World were to be dramatically reduced, whether through deliberate withdrawal or through Western economic collapse, the plight of developing countries would be even worse than at present. That is not to deny that much needs to be done to reform the workings of Western capitalist economies. There will however be opposition to this verdict, and this opposition will come from two quarters, from those who paint a rosier picture of our involvement or argue that reform is impracticable anyway, and from those who paint a gloomier picture and advocate withdrawal or revolution.

A 'conservative' Critique

First, there are many who would no doubt claim that the 'debit' features are neither as serious nor as widespread as is implied by the attention which has been paid to them. They might go on to say that in any case, given the clear weighting on the 'credit' side, we do in an overall way 'help' developing countries through our trade and investment, quite apart from any Aid we might give.[8] However, apart from not recognising the evident seriousness of the 'debit' side, this line of thought is somewhat complacent in that it fails to recognise the deeper logic of 'helping'. It must be apparent that one cannot rest content with 'overall helping'. For to help is to avoid harming the interests of others and hindering or preventing others from promoting their interests. It is no good saying that you are trying to help someone, if you also do things which hinder or harm him. If you are *serious* about helping, you do not help with one hand and hinder with the other. You try to co-ordinate the two hands into effective and consistent action.

To this the 'conservative' opponent will reply in two connected ways.

(i) The observation at the end of the paragraph may seem plausible but it is quite irrelevant. For it is just a fact that one must take the 'rough with the smooth'. The workings of any complex system such as Western capitalism have some unfortunate consequences. These consequences are the inevitable effects of the system, and though one can choose to adopt the overall system, it is not in human control to prevent all the bad consequences of its operation. (The same would apply to any other system, such as a centrall planned economy.)

(ii) But usually what lies behind the preceding claim is a rather deeper *moral* claim. A policy of 'helping', it may be said, is perfectly consistent with causing hardships, provided that such hardships are a side-effect of things which one does which one is either *entitled* to do or *obliged* to do for other moral reasons. Do we not accept, whatever our own point of view, that a Catholic may be serious and genuine in his intention to help a mother with a large family who does not want any more children, even though he will not condone, recommend or facilitate her taking artificial contraceptive measures *because he thinks it is wrong?* So it might be argued (and is certainly often assumed) that companies must have freedom to pursue their economic policies as they choose, even if they sometimes make immoral decisions. Or that companies have a duty to give high dividends to their shareholders. Or that Western Governments have a duty to pursue policies which promote the national interest or the living standards of their electorates.

To these two connected arguments the following all too brief replies may be given. The argument (i) that many bad consequences of economic activity are inevitable and not subject to human control is altogether defeatist. Human institutions and practices do get modified in the light of changing moral values and changing perceptions of self-interest. Consider the abolition of the slave trade or the dismantling of colonial empires in this century.

No doubt one reason for claiming that one must take the 'rough with the smooth' is the assumption that since 95% of our motivation, as it were, for being involved with developin

60

countries, is simply economic self-interest, the 'help' which we give by our economic involvement is not altruistic but simply a by-product of the pursuit of our own interests. It so happens that on the whole this self-interested policy benefits developing countries more than it harms them. But the harm done is just an inevitable consequence of economic self-interest. Given then this basic fact about human motivation, it is idealistic, in the sense of unrealistic, to suppose that pointing out the help/harm inconsistency will make any difference to practice, whether in general economic policies or in the nature of Aid programmes.

It is to be granted that if the assumption of the previous paragraph is correct and our only interest in relationships with developing countries is the promotion of our own interests, then indeed the whole analysis of 'help' would be beside the point. But if *part* of our interest stems from a genuine internationalism of outlook or a sense of community with other parts of the world, then helping will not merely be a by-product but also an objective. And it will follow that we will not only be concerned to improve the quality of our Aid, we will also want to reduce or eliminate the inconsistencies in our relationships whereby we give with one hand and take away with the other.

The tendency towards an overbearing concern for one's own interests, whether in individuals or in states, is perennial and powerful, as is the intellectual temptation to justify it in theories of egoism. One can only claim that other sources of motivation, from moral considerations, from altruistic concern, from a sense of international identity and so on, do exist and in some contexts effectively guide policy. No further argument for this is given here, since the whole book is really an attempt to demonstrate the existence of these effective sources of action.

The second argument (ii) against reform in Western economic activity also raises big moral issues. Anyone who really thinks that a company has a duty to its shareholders to pay the lowest possible wage to a Third World employee, or that our Government has a duty to its electorate to pursue British interests without regard for any moral constraints, has a very limited vision of the nature of moral responsibility. In particular he would have failed to acknowledge the force of the arguments advanced in the book. For any one who had acknowledged them, *just would not think* in these nationalistic or parochial terms. Anyone who claims that our serious obligation to help alleviate world poverty may be overridden by the kinds of observation just mentioned, thereby shows that he does not really believe that we have a serious obligation. They are just words, which have not sunk in.

A 'radical' Critique

On this analysis the balance sheet should read "Overall influence not beneficial". The bad consequences of Western involvement are not only greater than we have allowed, they are also irremovable, for they are the inherent features of Western culture in general or of Capitalism in particular.[9] Given this sort of analysis of the situation, there are broadly two kinds of response to it:
(a) The West should pull out of Developing Countries, and let them get on with their own development, since they would do better that way.
(b) Given that Capitalism, whether national or international is the chief impediment to social progress including the alleviation of poverty, the most effective thing to be done is to get rid of capitalism. Since Aid and attempts at reform make little difference to the essential tendencies of capitalism, and since those who control the system, whether in Western countries or non-communist developing countries, will never willingly transform the system from which they benefit, then the main focus must be upon revolution.

The first response (a) has its attractions though in the end it is in fact a dead end. It is tempting to think that if only developing countries freed themselves from Western models of development, rid themselves of the multinationals which exploit their natural resources and promote capital-intensive technology, and promoted their own goals in an autonomous self-reliant fashion, then they would solve many of their problems. Certainly greater ethnic independence and less reliance on Western cultural and economic models would be a good thing. But there is no getting away from various significant facts.
(i) Developing countries do not want to be isolated in this way. They are in any case inextricably part of the modern world, and would not have it otherwise.
(ii) Revitalising the world economy rather than trying to

run it down would seem to be in the interests of all countries concerned.

(iii)   It is quite unrealistic to suppose that a large scale disengagement could occur. The trend is otherwise, and maybe the making of a more secure world depends upon this trend. What is more practicable is that pressure be put on Governments, Companies and so on, to improve the way the international economic system works.

The Marxist position or more generally radical position (b) cannot be adequately discussed here. It is brought in to clarify by contrast the present approach, which is no doubt, by common standards radical enough. The attractions of the position rest on three related assumptions.

(i)   The extensive evils associated with capitalism can be attributed to the type of system it is, rather than to, say, the inherent tendencies towards selfishness and indifference towards others, which are liable to manifest themselves *whatever* the system.

(ii)   The envisaged alternative system in which the evil consequences of capitalism will be eliminated is really possible, not just an abstraction in the minds of idealists.

(iii)   The superior value of this alternative system of international economics and the probability of its emerging, rather than of something else emerging no better than or worse than what is being destroyed, is such as to justify the scale or cost of revolutionary transformation, economic disruption or sheer war.

All three of these propositions may be doubted. One does not, in doubting (i), have to deny the possibility - that is, the real possibility - of a better society in which the natural tendencies towards selfishness and indifference can be better limited than they generally are. But in accepting such a possibility, one can deny that such a society conforms either to actual or to envisaged communist models, or that it will emerge through violent revolution rather than through the quieter transformations in the minds and hearts of individual people. Be that as it may, the costs involved in any significant *collapse* (as opposed to reform) of our present world economic order would be of such a magnitude that they ought to give pause to any would-be revolutionary. It might, for all one knows, be the inevitable march of history that the captialist economic order collapses - and indeed it is at the very least a serious possibility that the combined effects of various global problems such as resource shortages, pollution and rampant militarism will cause such a collapse. But it is difficult to see how anyone, radical or otherwise, even if he hoped for or expected a new order to arise from the ashes, could hope for - let alone work for - the collapse of, rather than the serious but orderly reform of, the present international economic order. For such a collapse would be catastrophic for all concerned, not least developing countries, as the Brandt Report clearly recognises.

These criticisms of the conservative and radical approaches conclude the main part of this chapter, which has been concerned with issues raised by the 'capacity to help'. These issues are relevant to two kinds of argument which are sometimes used to support the basic contention that we have a substantial obligation to help alleviate world poverty. These arguments point to the same practical conclusion as the present arguments, but are not wholly acceptable. They nevertheless point up central issues and are worth a brief discussion. The first concerns distributive justice, the second corrective justice.

Forms of Egalitarianism

If one reflects upon the sorts of facts given earlier concerning the immense gap between the wealth and use of resources in rich countries and those of poor countries, one may be inclined to claim that the *gap itself,* quite apart from the extreme poverty which it involves, is unjust and ought not to exist. Now there are two ways in which this claim can be taken.

(a) One can adopt a hardheaded egalitarian stance and argue that *all* inequalities - at least in the basic goods of life which are subject to control - are wrong, and that a sustained attempt to reduce inequalities until basic equality is achieved should be given high moral priority. Thus the reduction of world poverty is a pressing obligation on this basis. Certainly, if one thought that this principle was fundamental in one's understanding of moral relations *within* a society, then in consistency the same principle would apply to relations *between* countries, and thus the whole of the gap would be subject to criticism *as such.* However it is not clear what the attractions of strict egalitarianism are. A society in which all are equal with

64

respect to distributable goods such as wealth and possessions is hardly attainable, let alone *sustainable*, were it somehow started by some magic wave of a wand.[10] In any case it is hardly desirable, since it is not necessary for and is probably an obstacle to the general achievement of the 'good life' or quality of life, and since such a society would lack much of the variety and diversity which enriches social existence.

(b) On the other hand, one can adopt a less hardheaded egalitarianism. For one may argue that the inequalities in a society or in the world are *too great* or of such a kind as to invite serious criticism and practical measures to reduce them. What one is really after is not total equality, simply less inequality. Many of those who call themselves 'egalitarians' and advocate egalitarian arguments, do in fact take this less extreme position. One might call it 'directional egalitarianism'. There is much to be said for directional egalitarianism, given the realities of the world, though the label 'egalitarian' has to be used cautiously because of the ambiguity involved.

If one adopts the second approach one is really relying on other moral arguments in the background. It is not the inequality as such which is wrong but what it in fact represents or points to. If one asks what is wrong with gross inequalities, as opposed to inequalities as such, or asks why certain inequalities are *too* great, one is immediately forced to look further. *Too* great by what standard? By the standard of justice, one may say. But now we need to know what that standard is and a further moral argument is drawn in. Thus gross inequalities may be a sign of injustice in the relations between the rich who are powerful and the poor who are weak. They may also be the sign of other forms of oppression such as religious or racial persecution and discrimination. It is obvious that great wealth confers great power, and thus wealth will breed injustices of the kind indicated, *unless* the power of wealth is curbed by constitutional democracy, by a well protected system of rights, and by rigorous legal checks on exploitative and discriminatory practices. Gross inequalities may also be a sign of social injustice in the very fact that a society does not *care* enough for its weakest members nor is prepared, through redistributive taxation and private generosity, to help alleviate poverty.

The upshot of this discussion then is that the reasons why the great gap between rich and poor countries is a matter for moral concern, are the reasons already advanced earlier. For our great wealth and their great poverty indicate both the existence of exploitative practices and also our general lack of concern to redistribute wealth precisely to alleviate extreme poverty. Insofar as the great gap signifies these factors, it symbolises a great evil in the world. On the other hand, it is sheer nonsense to suppose that *the whole of the gap* is a sign of wickedness. For this simply ignores the immensely complicated historical reasons for Western affluence, the time scale of the industrial revolution and so on. Nevertheless the gap leaves absolutely no room for moral complacency, for it points backwards to our past errors and omissions, and forwards to the challenge to which we must respond.

Inequality: the Racialist Factor

One of the things which the image of the great gap or divide between rich and poor countries tends to suggest is the possibility that racialism may play a significant if hidden role in influencing Western attitudes. Now it is no doubt a standard perception of the gap by Western thinkers to think that it is just an accident or contingent fact that on the whole the Rich West is White, and the Nations of the Third World are of other racial types. But thinkers in the Third World may wonder if it is just an accident or contingent fact. For they may suspect that one reason why Western countries have been exploitative or indifferent towards Third World poverty is simply that people in developing countries are of different race (and that if a poor country were White, it would get very different treatment, etc.). Now this accusation of racialism may come hard to Western ears, and it is important not to make too much of it. After all, if we are exploitative or indifferent, this may be due as much to general selfishness or to Nationalism as to specific racialist bias. Nevertheless, we must take seriously the charge that racialism may account for part of our overall inadequacies in relation to developing countries.[11]

We need to distinguish between explicit or conscious racialism and implicit or semi-conscious racialism. The systematic racialism of Apartheid in South Africa or the sporadic racialism of youths bashing up Blacks in our inner

66

cities are both examples of explicit racialism, however different in detail the two cases may be. On the other hand, the general tendency for people to give less weight to the moral claims of individuals, because they belong to a different race (or different sex, or different religion, or different class, etc.) is a manifestation of racism (or sexism, etc.). For example in job applications, the right to have relevant professional qualifications considered and not extraneous ones may be subtly abused by interviewing panels. And this form of implicit racialism, though it may not be blatant and may be largely unconscious, becomes, if it is widespread, a serious moral evil.

It is a serious moral question to ponder whether we collectively in the West are not guilty of racialist bias in our relations with developing countries. (We can put on one side the special issue of how far we are racialist in giving political support to a racialist government like South Africa.) Though we care to some extent through private charity or support for Government Aid, perhaps we would care rather more, if it was not for the fact that we think *sotto voce* - in fact so *sotto voce* that we do not hear ourselves think - "Since they are human, we must care, but they are racially different, so we need not care all that much...". Though those in business would of course generally profess to observing principles of justice in all their economic dealings, perhaps they are not quite so scrupulous or earnest about what they do, when it comes to a trade deal with a Third World country or when it comes to settling upon a wage level for peasant workers. Perhaps the thought, again *sotto voce*, occurs that it is after all Blacks they are dealing with. Honest self-examination might reveal that had they been White workers in an identical employment situation, the businessman would not have dreamt of making them accept such a low wage.

If such unconscious racial bias or indeed conscious bias is a significant feature of Western dealings with the Third World and accounts for part of what is wrong in our attitudes and practices, then it is a very serious matter. It is hardly the *main* cause of our moral failings, but it does seem to be a significant element in the picture. Such is the emotive power of an accusation of racialism, that any ascendancy in the perception of the North-South divide as a *racialist* divide, will do serious damage to future world

dialogue and progress, and will do little good for anyone.
It is therefore vitally important that the West does clearly
demonstrate that its policies and practices are not racialist
even in a small degree. This does mean changes of attitude,
for it is pretty clear that racial bias is a contributory
factor in accounting for why we do not do what we ought.
One piece of evidence for this is the fact that there is much
racial prejudice *within* countries such as Britain. It is
inconceivable that such prejudice should not affect the
attitude of people towards the Third World and towards the
seriousness of our responses to the plight of their poor.

Corrective Justice and Responsibility

Finally we need to look at another kind of reason that may
be advanced for the conclusion that we in the West ought to
do a lot to alleviate world poverty. The argument runs as
follows: Since we in the West are collectively responsible
for, in the sense of being to blame for, much of the poverty
in the World, we ought to make restitution for or give
compensation for what we have done - both in the colonial
and post-colonial periods. On this argument, what we ought
to do is based on the fact that we did or are doing something wrong, rather than on the fact that there is a terrible
situation which we ought to change. It may be granted that
one of the causes of the situation is what we have done up
to the present time: but the view that we have advocated
is that the basis for our moral response is the situation
itself plus our capacity to improve it. On the view being
considered it is what we have done which gives rise to the
obligation to make amends.

In one respect the argument is useful in that it points up
the fact that the moral inadequacies of the West lie not just
in our sins of omission or general indifference, but also
in our sins of commission, i.e. the various forms of active
injustice already referred to.[12] But the argument based on
compensation, making amends and so on seems to put the
emphasis in the wrong place. Talk about compensation or for
that matter 'punishment' for international sins is highly
problematic in this context. For it would give rise to
quasi-legal wrangling which is liable to deflect from the
main issue. There are problems about what the compensation
is for and how it could be measured. If poor people have
suffered or died, what constitutes repayment? If a man has

died, you cannot repay him, nor can the years of suffering be somehow wiped off the slate by a later improvement, as a debt is wiped out when it is paid. The whole notion of compensation seems out of place here. One needs a legal setting or an agreed frame of reference for such talk of corrective justice to get a firm conceptual foothold.

If we are talking about the issue in moral terms, the central point is that if we accept that we are or have been responsible for certain things, then we must accept that we ought not *to continue to do* those things for which we are responsible. This rests on the simple logical point that if I am to blame for doing something wrong up to now, it continues to be wrong for me to do it from now on (except for special circumstances). The recognition that I have been responsible for something wrong may be accompanied by regret or guilt but what is more significant is the will to do otherwise in the future. If we in the West were to do just that vis-à-vis our relations to developing countries, our attitudes and practices would be transformed - and it would be doubtful if anyone would see any point in talking about compensation. Indeed, even if some way of working out what it amounted to were available, it would turn out to involve *rather less* than what we are obliged to do anyway by the main arguments which have been deployed.

It is in any case counter-productive to talk in *general* terms of compensation, making amends and so on, for such talk will tend to put up the backs of would-be sympathetic people in the West. This is not to say that there are not *specific* areas in which the notion of legal compensation and the moral importance of its being achieved are appropriate. The case of the rights to compensation for American Indians comes to mind. And no doubt with the development of international law, it will become increasingly possible for companies and even countries to be found by an international court to be guilty of injustice or exploitation, and for compensations to be determined. This development is all to the good. But let us not imagine that it could rectify more than a very small part of the wrongs of the past. Nor could it, given the legal nature of the case, begin to call us to account for the wider sins of omission, our collective indifference and lack of concern, which form a significant part of our past failings.

The concept of responsibility looks, as it were, in two directions. We look to the past when we ask whether someone is or was responsible for having done something or let something happen. We attach blame when it ought not to have been done or have **happened.** We look forward when we specify what a person's responsibility or duty is, or what a responsible moral agent ought to do. Now the main focus of the moral arguments in this work is upon our prospective responsibilities upon what our *responses* ought to be to the tragic situation which we actually find in the world. It certainly does not follow, as a matter of strict logic, that if it is our responsibility to help alleviate the evil of poverty, then we are responsible for the existence of that evil. (If I come across an injured person needing help, it may be my responsibility to help him, though I certainly was not responsible for his injury.) But it so happens that in the present case, we have collectively been responsible for the existence of world poverty, or more strictly, for part of it. That is, we can be blamed for both our acts of commission and our acts of omission. For the actions and attitudes of Governments, companies and individuals can be criticised and can be said to be contributory 'causes' of world poverty.

It is then on this retrospective side to the notion of responsibility that we have focussed in the last few pages. However strange it may sound, there is a sense in which we in the West are 'responsible for' part of the poverty overseas and hence 'to blame' for it. And one can add to this the corollary: we continue to be responsible for this and hence to blame for it for as long as we fail to give adequate attention to our prospective responsibility to help alleviate that poverty. One aspect of this is that, if we ought to be less indifferent to such poverty, then we are responsible for the poverty that would have been eliminated as a result of our reduced indifference. But the point is not that we are responsible for all the poverty which we *could* have removed, but for all the poverty which we *would* have removed, had we done what we ought to have done. Whatever the case for a few individuals, there is little doubt that collectively we in the West are still responsible for the continued existence of much of the poverty in the world. And however unwelcome this verdict may seem, it is simply one of the consequences of the main arguments of this chapter. Let us then strive to be less responsible by becoming more responsible. That at any rate is the challenge.

70

Chapter 6

WORLD POVERTY AND WESTERN SELF-INTEREST

Two Arguments

In this chapter we will consider briefly a quite different
kind of argument which is often presented in favour of the
proposition that the West ought to do more to help with
development. This argument, briefly and starkly, is that it
is in our *interests* to do so. It is a significant feature of
the recently published Brandt Commission Report that it
stresses this point.[1] This is not because the Report is
sceptical about the importance of moral arguments - indeed
there is a deep moralism about the Report's commitment to
world community and international solidarity. Rather the
Brandt Commission were concerned that the arguments concerning self-interest had not been taken sufficiently seriously
by Western Governments and other large institutions. It is
perhaps a small irony that the Report was addressed primarily to Governments, but has been taken note of primarily
by individuals.

The arguments from self-interest fall roughly speaking into
two categories. First it is argued on fairly straight-
forward economic grounds, that greater development in
developing countries will benefit Western nations economically.[2] For greater development will mean greater wealth
which will be used to purchase goods from Western countries.
For example, quite apart from any moral arguments which one
may or may not accept against failing to stabilise international commodity prices and against pursuing protectionism
in order to stop the import of manufactures from developing
countries, there is the argument from self-interest that
unstable commodity prices and protectionist policies actually
damage our own overall economic interests.

The logic of this argument is more or less this. Suppose
that there is a more or less stable international economic
situation continuing into the foreseeable future; then a
scenario in which the West gives more Aid, stabilises
commodity prices, refrains from protectionism, etc., is
preferable on economic grounds to the one in which things
carry on much the same as they do at present. This argument
is, as it stands, a significant one, and it could no doubt
be applied to many areas of international economic activity.

It is however very controversial, in that economists may argue, in great technical detail, about the pros and cons of various policies.

The second category of argument however is more far-reaching and depends less on the refined judgments of experts to make an impact. For it questions the supposition made above. It supposes instead that the alternative to a programme of international economic reform directed at improving development in poorer countries, is *not* 'carrying on much as before', but rather the collapse of the world economy and dramatic increase in global tension and disarray. Such catastrophe may be either predicted as certain if we do not change our ways, or at least predicted as a serious possibility. Either way, the argument is that, since the alternative is *not* in our interests, economically, politically or any other way, it must be in our interests to strengthen the world economy and the bonds of international community, and the most effective way of doing this is to take numerous measures to lift poor countries from absolute poverty.[3]

This nightmarish scenario may become a reality largely through our not heeding the danger signals and our letting ourselves slide into it. This possibility is powerfully argued by Ronald Higgins in *The Seventh Enemy*; the seventh enemy being our intellectual and moral blindness to the six major global problems which he identifies as leading to global catastrophe. But it is worth adding that an important factor may be an increasing breakdown in communication between rich and poor countries. The 'North-South' Dialogue may turn into a 'North-South' confrontation and ultimately into global war.

One area where this may develop is over resources - an issue discussed in greater detail in Chapter 8. For if Western nations determined to maintain high flows of oil and mineral resources, put heavy economic pressure on developing countries or resort to military force to secure supplies, that will be a major destabilising development. Conversely if developing countries feel that their legitimate aspirations to take a greater share in development are being thwarted by Western intransigence, they may give up 'dialogue' as a farce and adopt an increasingly hostile attitude towards the West, (with the possibility of 'nuclear blackmail' not being ruled out).[5] And though a breakdown of such networks of cooperation would not serve the interests of developing countries, such a breakdown would be understandable, as an expression of their deep frustration and anger at what seems to them to be, and is, Western injustice.

It is clear that these arguments are important ones, and that they should be deployed, as arguments of persuasion, to support the same practical conclusions as the moral arguments already considered. However they are arguments which have to be handled with considerable caution, and give rise to several complications which need to be noted. First several points must be noted concerning the first level of argument, based on the calculation of economic advantage.

Genuine Development?

First, it is by no means clear that the detailed policies required by enlightened self-interest would coincide with the detailed policies required by moral reasoning. For the former might either fall short of or actually conflict with the latter. The Brandt Commission Report, whilst stressing the general idea of mutuality of interests, acknowledges that assistance to the very poorest, where the moral arguments are most powerful, is not so obviously supported by arguments of self-interest.[6]

This relates to a standard criticism made over the years of the types of transfer of financial resources mady by Governments in their Aid programmes and by Multinational companies in their investment policies. The critisicm is that the criteria for these transfers have been on the whole shaped by considerations of economic self-interest or national security, rather than considerations concerning development as such, particularly development for the poorest people in developing countries. Thus Aid is 'tied' to the purchase of the manufactures of the donor country or to the employment of experts from the donor country, and projects may be adopted which are capital-intensive in situations where labour-intensive projects would actually help poor people much more. It comes down to which question is asked (or asked first):

(a) What ways of spending finance available for development are *best for genuine development* for poor people, irrespective of whether these policies and projects are *most* effective in promoting our economic interests, compared with other policies and projects?

(b) What policies of financial involvement, amongst the
various policies all of which happen to some extent to
support development and can therefore be 'justified' *in the
name of development,* will be *most* effective in promoting
our economic (or strategic or political) interests?

These two questions, which need to be faced primarily by
those influencing or administering Aid policies in rich
countries but also significantly by governments in Third
World countries themselves, are quite different in two
respects. First there is the more explicit difference of
priority in the intention: Are you after development or are
you after economic advantage? But there is also a difference
in the conception of what development is. Is development
thought of in terms of the improvement of the lives of poor
people, or thought of in terms of an increase in the G.N.P.
which may of course make no difference to, or even make things
worse for, the really poor?

It is clear that the projects and policies which one would
support could be significantly different, depending upon
which of the two questions one answered, and that there are
grounds for cynicism if what is done in the name of development is in fact determined by answers to the second question.

It does not incidentally follow automatically that once the
two questions are distinguished, a rich country must, morally
speaking, *only attend,* in its Aid giving or more generally
in its overall economic relations with poor countries, to
the first question, never to the second. Countries, no less
than individuals, are justified to some extent in promoting,
or at least protecting, their interests. But this justification is only available in the context of wider moral
considerations, including importantly our obligations to
poorer countries. And this means that the first question
must be taken seriously and in the case of Aid giving taken
first, with its answers given priority. Indeed a financial
transfer cannot be *thought of* by any honest thinker as Aid
or Development Finance - whatever it is *called* - if it is
not primarily a response to the first and not the second
question.

Morality and Self-Interest

This leads to the second point: suppose there is a conflict

between self-interest and morality. What does one advocate? It is clear that reasons of morality take precedence over reasons of self-interest: that is, one should only advocate self-interest as a legitimate reason for doing anything provided that so doing is acceptable from one's moral point of view. It is on this condition and with this understood that one advocates policies on the grounds of self-interest. It must not be denied that the fact that something promotes one's interests is one of the considerations which enters one's moral thinking about what to do. But the point remains that, if moral considerations show that not pursuing one's interests is required, then self-interest offers no legitimacy and one cannot advocate it for others in like circumstances.

Nevertheless, the dangers of using the 'self-interest' argument must be recognized. For the natural tendency implicit in using self-interest as an argument for persuading others, is that it acquires a legitimacy of its own, and the 'right to pursue one's self-interest' is regarded as a powerful and overriding consideration against moral concern for others. The inherent danger therefore of employing arguments from self-interest is that the person whom you are trying to persuade may turn round and point out that actually a different course of action is recommended by self-interest and that therefore you can hardly object to his not doing what you set out to recommend. And if you have to accept his factual assessment about self-interest you make your argument hostage to factual fortune. The danger of compromising the importance of the moral arguments can only be averted if one makes it clear *from the start* that one is only advocating self-interest within the moral framework.

This relates to a further point about what is implied by the phrase 'in one's interests' or 'in one's country's interests'. Does it imply that whatever is advocated promotes one's interests *more than* any other course of action? That is, that it 'maximises' one's interests? Or does it merely imply that whatever is advocated promotes one's interests, as opposed to frustrating them, or promotes them *as much as* continuing to do as one has done before? Now in the latter two senses, it might be true that, for instance, Britain's interests are still served if her economy grew at, say, 3% as opposed to 5% per annum, because more financial assistance is given to developing countries, or if through not engaging in protectionism, as many jobs were gained in one industry as were lost in another. Nevertheless, such policies might not be in Britain's interests in the first sense.

If on the one hand one is hardheaded about pursuing self-interest, one will be interested in it in the 'maximising' sense only and one will not pursue development policies which could only be recommended in the non-maximising senses. But in that case, one has rejected altogether the priority of moral argument and the general line of thought of this book. If on the other hand one is not hardheaded about the pursuit of self-interest, one may advocate its pursuit in the non-maximising senses. In that case one accepts that appeals to self-interest occur within the context of moral considerations and indeed do not really work except in conjunction with some moral concern or objective. Often the function of the appeal to self-interest is to show that one's interests are not seriously *damaged* by pursuing a moral end: but the positive initiative for action comes from the interest one has in the moral end. Concern, whether in an individual or in a country, over not damaging one's interests seems to be, unlike a drive to maximise one's interests, a perfectly legitimate consideration within the moral framework - even if there are some occasions when sacrifice is morally called for.

The Problem of the 'Free Rider'

A further observation concerning self-interest also reveals the close connection between appeals to self-interest and some moral consideration lying in the background. It concerns what is sometimes called in moral philosophy the problem of the 'free rider', someone who accepts the benefits of living in a society which come from people's observing rules of behaviour, but fails to observe them himself, thereby eating his cake and having it. If we talk generally of how it is in the West's interests to give more financial assistance and avoid protectionism, we leave open the following possibilities. Let us suppose that all Western nations do so except, let us say without pointing accusing fingers, Britain; that developing countries' economies flourish; and that there is more trade with all Western nations including Britain. In this case Britain eats her economic cake and has it. Conversely, let us suppose that Britain saw the sense of the West doing what has been suggeste and did its part. However no other countries did the same, and what little extra trade there is is spread over other countries as well. Here Britain would be economically the loser, even if she would have stood to gain had all the other countries done the same as her.

The consequence of this argument, which may come as a surprise, is this. If it is the case that Britain would only gain from a given policy *if* other Western nations followed the same policy, then one of two things might be the case. (i) Either Britain pursues it without any agreement with other countries: in which case the reason for her action is that she ought to *do her part* in pursuing a common good - and this is a moral argument, not a purely self-interested one. (ii) Or Britain pursues it because Western nations come to an agreement to pursue that policy, in which case Britain is not just pursuing her interests, she is fulfilling her obligation under the agreement. Either way a moral argument is invoked. Pure self-interest might lead to quite different policies. It is worth observing that it is because countries are worried about giving Aid and then not getting an economic return, that there is the overwhelming temptation to make Aid *tied,* that is, linked to obligations to trade with and use the professional services of the donor country.

It is often assumed that arguments concerned with self-interest have a down-to-earth realism to them, unlike moral arguments which have an up-in-the-clouds idealism about them. The former determine conduct, the latter influence sentiment. More will be said about the *practical* force of moral argument later, but if anything in the preceding discussion is sound, it should at least be clear that moral thought tends to enter the very texture of prudential reasoning to a far larger extent than appears at first sight. It also enters our understanding of what our interests are in more subtle ways as well, as may become clear in what follows concerning the second category of argument concerning self-interest.

Self-Interest and Global Identity

The second argument that unless the nations of the world cooperate to revitalise the world economy by giving substantial help to developing nations, then the serious collapse of the world order is likely, is a disturbing one, but it is probably sound in its general message. The trouble is that its message is so dramatic that it may shock nations into immobility, rather than galvanise them into reform. It may, or rather the growing crises which point to it may, incline nations to retreat into their shells and salvage what little of their interests they can protect, rather than to strive for cooperation and the international approach which is needed. What factors are relevant to determining how nations or individuals react to such dramatic challenges? Clearly much depends on how the probabilities of various developments are assessed, how likely it is that other countries will cooperate in policies which will only work if everyone plays their part and so on. However, the most significant factor lies elsewhere, namely in how countries (or individuals whose attitudes collectively shape those of countries) *conceive of* their interests or prudence. It is these conceptions which influence the kinds of assessments of the probabilities which one makes anyway.

Though there are numerous possible combinations of attitude, two 'ensembles' of attitude which identify different conceptions of self-interest are worth noting. Let us first consider this at the level of individuals. On the one hand, someone may have an attitude of caution: he is defensive and on the retreat, suspicious of others' intentions, not leaving anything to chance, intensely concerned about the security of his posessions, never engaging in a joint venture unless he is quite sure that the others are going to deliver the goods, and concerned purely with his own welfare and that of those immediately around him. On the other hand, someone may have an attitude of openness and trust towards others, not be preoccupied with the security of his possessions, generally assume others will cooperate in common ventures, be prepared to take bold steps and tackle problems in a spirit of hope, and be concerned in a general way with the welfare of humankind. Now these two sets of attitudes do reflect different conceptions of 'one's interests'. Consider how someone of the second kind would react to a situation in which cooperation was made impossible, those around him ceased to be open, friendly or trusting. He would feel that his good or what he valued in life was destroyed or at least partly so. Whereas the person with the first set of attitudes, though he would find it inconvenient, would not find his good significantly affected.

Now all this may seem far removed from the main topic: how do nations react to the possibility of international catastrophe? And yet it seems to have a distinct bearing. For the tendency to retreat into one's national shell, and advance nationalistic reasons to justify it, is partly a product of how that nation identifies itself, or how its citizens conceive of themselves. If they value trust and cooperation with other nations (and they like to think of themselves in this light), then they will be more prepared to search for common solutions to common problems, more ready to trust in others' playing their part, and so on.

The readiness to cooperate (at any level) depends as much on the perceived intrinsic value of cooperation as an ideal of human existence, as upon the particular advantages that may accrue from it on a particular occasion. It depends partly upon one's tendency to think of oneself as a member of the world and not just a member of a given nation. Moral reasons are often given for thinking in terms of world citizenship, but the important point is that if such a concept is a psychological reality for one, then one cannot help identifying one's interests partly in terms of one's positive rather than negative relation to that world. One will be reluctant to advocate policies which pull that world apart.

Advocates of global policies will often talk of considering one's long-term as opposed to short-term interests, and no doubt most people would accept that it would be in our long-term interests to have global cooperation, common policies, etc. But it remains an ideal abstraction, a 'would be' goal rather than an actual goal. This is partly because of the uncertainty of the future and the real possibility of economic collapse, nuclear war, environmental catastrophe, and so on. But it is also partly because there is little value placed on the intrinsic value of world community and unity, and correspondingly little boldness to strive for what one values, despite the risks. To persuade a man to take his long-term interests seriously and not just consider his short-term interests is not primarily a matter of persuading him of a set of facts, it is a matter of persuading him to adopt a new perspective, a new set of values and the will to pursue them. It is literally to encourage him.

It is also a matter of giving him or encouraging in him the attitudes of hope and caring, of responding positively to the possibility of good and working towards this rather than responding negatively to the dangers and possibilities of evil and thus reacting defensively through fear.

The argument then that it is in our interests to engage in global cooperation in order to avoid catastrophe is a sound one, but it is an incomplete one. For it will make no sense to anyone who does not have the necessary attitudes. These attitudes are partly the attitudes of internationalism itself and of a sense of global unity and identification, and partly the attitudes of caring, hope, courage and trust as general traits of character. Without the combination of these attitudes, it is likely that the way individuals and nations identify their interests in a world in crisis will tend to work against rather than for global cooperation.

In the end it is a matter of moral values. For the attitudes outlined are themselves impregnated with moral values. It is only people with certain moral values who adopt this combination of attitudes. What is more, if one is to convince people of the argument from self-interest for global cooperation, one must employ moral arguments, not only to show the need to adopt an international approach and to identify oneself as a citizen of the world, but also to show the importance of the basic attitudes of love, trust, hope and courage as moral virtues themselves. And all this of course lies beyond straight forward appeals to self-interest.

Whether or not nations have developed sufficient of the international approach to take the bold approach as opposed to the self-defeating course of caution remains to be seen. All one can do is stress the importance of the concept of international community and of the global approach to moral issues which has been an assumption behind the whole chapter. The upshot of our discussion then is that the arguments from self-interest, though important must be seen clearly in the moral context, which partly provides restraints upon economic self-interest and partly provides the content for wider conceptions of self-interest.

The Role of the Individual

It is worth concluding this chapter with a brief

examination of how the preceding arguments relate to the individual. It might be thought that if a policy of, say, financial assistance is in Britain's economic interests, it is in the interests of individuals in Britain to support such a policy and indeed make a financial contribution to development himself. This turns out not to be so.

Suppose for the sake of argument, that it *is* in Britain's economic interests to give more financial assistance in the form of Aid and of private giving and to avoid protectionism. Suppose also, to imagine an unreal abstraction, that someone is convinced by these arguments but *not by the moral arguments,* and he (a) gives money to overseas charities (b) writes to MPs urging more Aid and non-protectionism or joins an action group and gives talks, does leafletting, etc. We now ask the question: Is it in *his* economic or more generally materialistic interests to do these things? And the answer must surely be 'no' (in any normal circumstances). For if he does (a), then, in the absence of a general level of giving to the same degree, *he* will be financially worse off; if he does (b), then he devotes to these activities, time, effort and no doubt money which might have been devoted to his private interests, for instance, hobbies, amusements, maintenance of house, garden or car, or making more money.

He may do all these things then, simply because he thinks that *if* the Government does what he urges and *if* other people do as he does, then everyone, himself included, will benefit economically (for the reasons given earlier). But, *his* doing these things does not actually benefit *him* economically. For if other people are not doing what he is doing, then the shared benefits are not going to come. But if on the other hand, other people *were* generally being more generous (and the Government were doing more), it would again be in his economic interests to do nothing, since he could be a 'free rider' and share in the general benefits without doing anything himself. But, you may say, the last course of action would be unfair or immoral, since he ought to play his part. Quite. This is the general point. Any individual who sees something to be in the interests of a wider whole or group of which he is a part, normally promotes it out of some sense of moral obligation, some sense of moral commitment to the good of the whole, the good in which he will only share if others generally do their part as well.

It is of course true that a kind of self-interest comes into the picture when such a person devotes time, effort and money to something like this, but it is not economic and material-istic self-interest. For there is a kind of *satisfaction* which comes from doing these things.[7] But the point remains that this satisfaction *derives* from and depends upon the recognition that one is doing what one ought to do, or playing one's part. The personal commitment inevitably has a *moral* dimension. This is another reason why the arguments for self-interest advanced earlier in the chapter are in the end parasitic upon a firm moral sense. For no changes in Government practice or general attitude will come about (however potent the self-interest argument is in the abstract) unless *some individuals* put a lot of time, effort and money into promoting these changes - that is, time, effort and money which for them as individuals does not represent, and goes well beyond, any calculations of economic self-interest.

That is why the image of someone promoting the self-interest argument alone is an unreal abstraction. For no one would promote it without a strong moral sensitivity and this would almost inevitably include acceptance to some degree of the moral arguments for helping other countries anyway. At any rate, the arguments for convincing individuals to promote such help cannot rely on considerations of economic self-interest alone. For even if you convince someone of the self-interest arguments given in this chapter, you still have to get *him* to take a lead or take the moral plunge.

Chapter 7

WORLD POVERTY AND THE ENVIRONMENT

Divergence or Convergence?

What issues are raised when we consider the relationship between concern about world poverty and concern about the environment? This topic needs to be faced because there is a tendency for those concerned with the environment either to ignore or to reject the perspective of those concerned with world poverty. However a coherent overall perspective which embraces both sets of concerns is possible and indeed essential.

At the level of practical policies and popular arguments, the picture is indeed a confusing one. On the one hand, thinkers can be seen as pulling in different directions. Environmentalists are concerned with *our future* and that of our children, Developmentalists with the situation of *the poor of the world now*. Environmentalists usually advocate 'no growth' policies and putting the brakes on material consumption and on the use of natural resources and energy, whereas Developmentalists insist that poor countries need all the growth they can achieve and expansion in the use of their resources. Environmentalists tend to focus on the population explosion as a main cause of global problems and emphasise birth control programmes, whereas Developmentalists see Western affluence as a main cause of global problems, and regard birth control programmes as of secondary importance compared with development schemes themselves.[1]

On the other hand, there are things in common as well. Both groups are agreed at least on the negative point that much needs to be changed in Western attitudes and policies. They can agree on the need for us in the West to live less affluently and less wastefully. They can agree that technologies need to be 'appropriate' to genuine social needs, and that sophisticated capital-intensive technologies are often not right, whether in poor countries or rich countries. They can agree that greater control needs to be exercised over multinational companies, insofar as these may exploit both human and natural resources. They may agree also that greater self-sufficiency and self-reliance would be, at least in the long run, healthy for both rich and poor countries.

Whether the differences or the similarities are emphasised

depends of course upon the approach of the thinker, on how much he knows, where his heart lies, and what his set of values is. Different approaches do of course reflect the different *factual* assessments which thinkers may make of the environmental situation. These may range from a complete rejection of the idea that there is an environmental 'crisis' or global problem, to an attitude of doomsday pessimism. Far more significant however are the differences of *value* and moral approach which inform the way a person generally perceives the world around him and which have a strong influence upon the kind of 'factual' assessment a person make anyway. The discussion which follows deals with these broad differences of value perspective.

The 'Back to Nature' Approach

Let us first of all look at what may be called the 'Back to Nature' approach. In its extreme form this involves a rejection of Western technology, bureaucracy and the life-styles of affluence, and an acceptance of - usually perceived as a return to - simple life-styles. A central idea is that one should live in harmony with one's ecological milieu, and go in for things like organic farming, herbal medicines, traditional crafts, and generally a greater degree of self-sufficiency for individuals or for small social groups like communes. Such life-styles appeal to those who try them not just because they see them as environmental 'good sense', but also because they hold the key to the 'good life', to the sor of life that is worth living anyway.[2]

No doubt to most people who are well stuck in their patterns of affluence, there is either a certain Romanticism about it all, or else a sheer crankiness: for them it is not really worth seriously bothering about. However there is much of value in the practices and life-styles of such groups and individuals, provided they are perceived and presented in a certain light. What is this proviso? It is that these practices are seen as examples of what can be done in an extreme form so as to encourage most people to do the same sorts of things in a limited form, i.e. to be less wasteful, less polluting and less bound by the assumptions of affluence If on the other hand these practices are presented as a universal way of life for everyone, then most ordinary think-ing people will simply dismiss such life-styles as beyond the rational pale, rather than see them as ideals pointing to som of the changes which we all ought to make.

Now undoubtedly the way many people react to the 'simple life
style' approach does depend upon a failure of communication
on the part of those committed to it. It is fair to add
however that many of those who are committed to such life-
styles would dispute the present analysis of their value and
role in the total picture. For they maybe involved in an
uncompromising rejection of ordinary ways of life, including
moderate attempts to live less wastefully. If so, the 'back
to nature' approach needs to be criticized.

First, it is simply unrealistic to suppose that we can
generally turn our backs on technology, on urban living and
the complexity of its organisation, or on the undoubted
benefits and cultural riches gained through universal
education, universal health care or professions in the arts.
And we must not forget that in large measure these benefits
owe their existence to the surplus wealth created by the
production of material goods. We need to recognise that
there is an immense range of possible approaches towards
technology, between the common worship of modern technology
and an uncompromising rejection of technology. What is
needed is a critical appraisal of the uses of technology, of
what to use and what not to use, of what to develop and what
not to develop. We need, that is, 'appropriate'
technologies. All the word 'appropriate' does is to make us
ask the question "What is technology appropriate for".[3] It
is not an end in itself, but serves human ends, good, bad or
indifferent, as we choose or as we all too often just let
happen.

Moral One-sidedness

But the reason for looking at this 'back to nature' form of
conservationism first of all is that it often illustrates a
certain kind of moral approach, which tends to be adopted
by those generally in the counter-cultures of community
living and so on. For there may be a certain moral one-
sidedness about it all. There is often a kind of inward-
looking attutude, an isolationism and a turning away from the
wider world, from one's own country and a *fortiori* from the
fortunes of people in other countries. Thus this approach,
whether explicitly or implicitly, does not accept a dimension
to moral responsibility, according to which individuals or

groups stand in moral relations to other individuals or groups far removed from them, e.g. the poor of the Third World.

The attitude rests on several factors. First, it is not surprising that, with the rejection of materialistic values, great emphasis is put upon the values of genuine community and of personal relationships. However, though these values are important and we need more recognition of them in our society, they are not so important that they should become the sole *locus* of moral consciousness. The networks of social relationships in which we stand morally toward others are vast, and extend in all directions around the personal relations and close community with which the *felt* quality of life may often be identified. Thus insofar as a preoccupation with this quality of personal living blurs one's perception of the wider moral networks with which it is interwoven, there is cause for concern.

Another source for an inward-looking attitude, and not always distinguished from the first, comes from a certain attitude towards nature as a whole.[4] 'Nature' becomes an object of reverence. Animal and plant life is to be respected as far as possible, and we are to live in harmony with Nature and in ecological balance with the rest of creation. Is this attitude sound?

On the one hand, it does seem clear that we do stand in some kind of direct moral relation to Nature, at least to 'living' nature. There are, and ought to be recognised, certain moral constraints in our treatment of living beings, which derive from their nature as living beings, and not from the indirect consequences for human beings. Animals have rights, at least in the sense that it is wrong to kill or inflict pain on animals without serious cause. Even plants and trees can be said to possess characteristics which impose moral constraints on our behaviour. It would surely be wrong to destroy a tree for no good reason at all, quite apart from such an act's being wasteful in relation to human needs or expressive of immoderate mental attitudes or impulses, as in the case of vandalism. Furthermore there is much of practical importance in the idea of living in 'harmony' with nature rather than constantly upsetting ecological patterns. For we disrupt these patterns at our collective peril. It is also true that living in the constant awareness of the rhythms, patterns and cycles of nature is psychologically healthy, and would be so for many who do not recognise the fact because they live in cities which largely cut people off from such awareness.

On the other hand, what is worrying about this way of looking at things is that it is liable to displace or dislodge our moral values concerning our fellow human beings. If the important thing in one's life is to get into the right relation with Nature, then it may cease to be important that one get into the right relations with fellow human beings in general. It is almost as if one can look in two directions, *vertically* towards Nature, and *horizontally* towards fellow human beings, but one cannot look in both directions. There is an implicit 'either or' - as though the big bad world of human affairs is of no concern, provided one is properly tuned into one's ecological wavelength. The correct response to this picture is to say that any regard for nature must be integrated into a proper social morality, in which one has a concern for human beings and their welfare, and not just those with whom one has direct dealings.

Indeed it must be noted that many of those who advocate simple life-styles do have an explicit social morality, and more specifically, do have a concern for world poverty. And they may very well argue that their advocacy of simple life-styles, simpler technologies, organic farming methods and so on, is not relevant just to their own lives, but has application to the problems of the Third World as well. One may withdraw to one's croft, but this is no moral withdrawal, since one advocates policies which have perfectly general validity.

If someone with the 'back to nature' approach develops this line of thought, there are three broad options which he might take:
(a) Though poor people would do well to lead a qualitatively simple life, i.e. one that is neither like their present extremity of poverty nor like the typical patterns of Western affluence, it is of no interest to *him* to do anything about helping to bring it about.
(b) The best thing that we in the West can do is to do nothing, to withdraw from contact with developing countries, and to let them get on with appropriate development without

interference from us.

(c) Though he, the advocate of simple life-styles, is doing nothing directly to help alleviate world poverty, because he has chosen the symbolic stance of simple living, there is much that needs to be done by Governments and other people who have not taken his stance and have not withdrawn from affluence.

Of the three positions, option (c) has most to commend it. For whilst the stance of simple living is seen as a significant *part* of the whole picture, the alleviation of world poverty as an important moral goal is also given full recognition. So long as the advocate of the simple life-style sees this goal of reducing poverty as an essential part of his own overall moral position and not just an implicit footnote to it, it cannot be quarrelled with. But insofar as he is liable to adopt options (a) or (b), then there is much to quarrel with.

For option (a) indicates a failure or unwillingness to see morality in a certain crucial way, a failure which is by no means restricted to those whom we are considering now. It depends upon failing to make the transition from the fact that something ought objectively to exists to the fact that in principle one ought, if one can, to promote its existence. This failure is of course a blindness to which we are all at times susceptible; the error lies in its becoming a settled lack of perception or a declared policy of egoism.

Option (b) on the other hand depends on a seriously incorrect assessment of the *facts* of our global situation. For it depends upon an extraordinarily gloomy assessment of the negative effects of Western involvement in poor countries. There is no doubt that our involvement could be *much* better; no doubt too that *in the long run* greater self-sufficiency would be beneficial for poorer countries. But the suggestion that neither the present mix of policies nor any improved mix of policies of active involvement would be as helpful as total withdrawal, appears to be very far-fetched. Such withdrawal would be neither desirable nor indeed practicable, and no adequate moral position is possible unless it includes an account of *how* the West should be involved with developing countries, and also how conservation objectives affect the general character of international policies and goals. To that we must now turn, having indicated the attractions and drawbacks of the semi-Romantic withdrawal back to Nature.

The Need for Global Conservation Strategies

Many of those concerned with environmental issues do of
course see them in global terms, and with a deep sense of
moral commitment and reforming zeal, advocate new codes of
conduct for people in general, new policies for Governments,
new directions and areas for initiative in internationally
agreed objectives. Works like *Limits to Growth* painted a
stark picture of a finite world, of the finiteness of
resources and energy supplies, the finiteness of the earth's
food and vegetation growing capacities, and the finite
capacity of the biosphere to absorb pollution from
effluents, pesticides and fertilizers.[5] A first and natural
reaction to such bleak facts must be: Let's reach for the
global handbrake fast!

Many have argued that the initial diagnoses or scenarios of
works such as *Limits to Growth* were too pessimistic - or
merely geared to shock us into action. But the fact remains
that the world is a finite place. Even if technology does
find solutions for its own polluting tendencies and does
invent substitutes for scarce resources, and vast new mineral
and energy sources do keep on being discovered, there are
limits somewhere. The finiteness of the world's resources,
of its pollution-absorbing capacities and of its areas for
producing renewable resources, this finiteness is a *quite
definite necessity.* The perception of this finiteness as a
practical constraint on decision-making will not ever go
away, even if decision-makers still pretend it is not there
to see. Furthermore, the fact remains that we do not know
how far technology and the discovery of resources will be
able to cope with increasing material demands. To put all
one's faith in technology and not to question our ways of
affluence shows all the signs of a dangerous addiction. It
is sometimes called the 'technological fix'.

The first natural reaction then is one of wanting to put the
brakes on. The natural orientation for this is thought of
the future, perhaps not the indefinite future but that expanse
of the future which has some psychological reality for us.
The future means that small stretch of the future in which we
expect to grow old and in which we expect our children, our
children's children and more generally those whom we care for

89

to go on living. In terms of this future-oriented perspective, one considers what policies are needed on a global scale in order to secure a reasonable future for Mankind. In the name of this moral objective - man's collective future well-being - one will be inclined to advocate 'no growth' policies, strict or limited use of fertilisers and pesticides, birth control programmes, limited use of, if not outright rejection of, nuclear energy, preservation of wildernesses such as large forests, encouragement of public transport systems, discouragement of private motor cars and vast capital expenditure associated with them, extensive energy conservation measures, greater research into solar energy, and so on.[6]

There is much to commend in such measures; and particularly in the attempt to find global answers. For any solution to problems which is given in the name of morality must be given from a global or international point of view. And this is what is attempted here. Nevertheless, there is the danger that some of those who think in these terms will produce a one-sided set of prescriptions on a global scale. The danger of course lies in the fact that in the name of our collective future, one may overlook the well-being of human beings who *here and now* live in great and extreme poverty, and for whom this single-minded zeal for the future may seem like a sick joke or cruel irony. And let us remember that there are over 800 million people who live here and now in extreme poverty. The joke is *very* sick and the irony *very* cruel.

It is surely obvious that, whether or not the kind of affluence presently existing in Western countries is either possible or desirable for all poor countries, poor countries need *considerable* growth in the use of resources and energy if they are to escape the afflictions of absolute poverty. Poor countries need more artificial fertilisers and pesticides, if they are to increase food production adequately. And so on. The environmentalist's argument is set out in terms of the future of Mankind or of our collective future well-being. But if those advocates are not seriously concerned with the *present* well-being of the poor in the world now, *whose* future are they really concerned about? It is highly counter-intuitive to suppose that they are concerned with the welfare of poor people in the future, if they are not concerned with it now in the total set of policies which they advocate for the world.

Thus an environmentalist global perspective, unless it is tempered by the arguments of developmentalists, is for all its 'internationalist' point of view liable to be a covert projection of concern for Western interests - or the interests of those better off in western societies - and thus smacks of Western chauvinism. We have another example of the metaphor of 'vertical and horizontal'. For within the general moral concern for the welfare of human beings, one can distinguish looking vertically (along the time axis as it were) towards the welfare of human beings in the future, and looking horizontally (along the geographical space axis) towards the welfare of human beings all over the world now. Again there is a tendency for people to focus their moral thinking along one or other of the axes. But it is a tendency to be resisted. For we need to look in both directions.[7]

Two kinds of attitude associated with concern for the environmental crisis have been considered. Both attitudes are valuable if set in wider contexts. Yet there is a danger that they may both be inadequate. The 'disengaging' return to nature and simple living may show an inadequate recognition of the demands of a wider social morality and a *fortiori* of a global social morality. The 'engaging' advocacy of global solutions and policies may show an inadequate appreciation of the nature of the moral demands made in the name of improving the material lot of the poor of the world now.

The Just and Sustainable Society

How then can the environmental and developmental perspectives be combined and an appropriate moral framework developed? First of all it is useful to introduce a label for this combined approach, namely the 'just and sustainable society' or, to be more precise the 'just and sustainable *global* society'.[8] But we can start with the basic idea of a just and sustainable society and then extend the idea into the global context.

It is already a very significant phrase when it applies only to a 'society' as we ordinarily conceive of it. For it reminds us, when we are thinking about what kind of a society we want in our own country, that if we are rightly

91

concerned with various measures needed in order to sustain our society into the future, we must not forget that such a society must be guided by the basic principles of justice and more generally by moral values which make life *worth* living. If the idea of a sustainable society as our goal recommends itself as a focus for our environmental concerns, we must also take care to ensure that it is the idea of a society which is *worth* sustaining, not just capable of being sustained. One function of the word 'just' here is simply to remind us of this general point about how to interpret 'sustainable'. Another function of the word 'just' is to highlight the importance of justice amongst moral values, as the conceptual vehicle for conveying the most exacting of moral demands, and as, in Rawls' phrase, the 'first virtue of institutions'.

There is much controversy of course about the nature of justice. Since a more theoretical justification of my approach was given earlier, a few brief remarks will suffice here. First what makes a society a 'just society' is not only the particular actions of individuals in relation to other individuals or groups of individuals, but also the basic structural features of that society, its laws, central institutions, established rights and practices. Furthermore, the ultimate assessment of how just a society is depends not simply on the internal relationships of people or on the internal consequences of institutions and practices within a society, but also upon the external relationships and consequences in relation to other societies and individuals and groups within them. But looking first at the 'internal' features of justice in a society, we can usefully group these into three areas and relate them to the idea of sustainability.

(i) The institutional principles of justice should include the maintenance of the basic liberties of a free society – such liberties as political freedom, freedom of speech, freedom of association, freedom to practice one's religion and so on. It is worth adding here one that is not so commonly emphasised, freedom from undue interference by bureaucracy. Any argument to the effect that the only way we can solve our environmental problems and get on course for sustainability is to abandon democracy for totalitarian control is highly suspect. This is partly on the practical grounds that 'centralist' or essentially bureaucratic solutions would be unlikely to work. For what the problems really require are flexibility, decentralisation and greater local autonomy. But it is suspect partly because, if you throw out freedoms such as these, much of what makes one's society worth sustaining has gone as well.

(ii) Equally important, though often under-recognised by self-styled liberals, are the basic rights or freedoms, summarised in the idea of freedom from want or the right to a decent way of life. Such a right brings along in its wake a whole cluster of more specific rights to the conditions appropriate to its realisation – the right to adequate food, health care, education, shelter, clean water, participation in the life and culture of the local community, and external circumstances for self-respect. In Chapter 4 we saw that the provision of these things should be seen as something required by *social justice*. A civilised society would at any rate care for the welfare of its members and take steps to make the necessary provisions. In a modern state this means in large measure the apparatus of the welfare state, which is financed by direct or indirect taxation of those with more wealth. Given this basic notion of social justice, we can see that any solutions proposed by environmentalists which involve for instance stopping growth or cutting down on material consumption, must pay particular attention to questions of social justice. For it is unreasonable to expect those who are poorest to accept reductions in their standard of living. Questions of redistribution become much more pressing when the cake remains the same size or gets smaller, than when it is getting bigger and there is the hope that everyone will get more, even without redistributive measures.

(iii) Principles of justice also include principles concerning commercial transactions, which provide the ethics of business and economic dealings, whether it applies to individuals, companies or governments. Thus contracts should not be made on the basis of misleading information or under undue pressure because of unequal economic strength, contracts should be honoured, and so on. Again any environmentalist solutions which attempted to ride roughshod over the accepted standards for business dealings would be questionable as well as no doubt unworkable.

These aspects of justice take on a new significance when we

turn to the wider concept of a 'just and sustainable global society'. For if our goal is to have a world which is worth sustaining, it must be a world made up of societies which are worth sustaining and in which the lives of human beings are generally worth living. Clearly the principles of justice mentioned above are relevant here, especially the second. For it is clear that in a world with 800 million absolute poor whose basic needs are not met, it is not really a question of how we can sustain a world in which life is generally worth living, it is a question of *creating* such a world. So if we are committed to sustaining a world worth sustaining, we must *a fortiori* be committed to creating such a world to be sustained. It is also clear that a world worth sustaining is one in which there are generally political and civic liberties, and a fair degree of autonomy for regions and communities. It is one in which economic transactions are generally conducted in fair and reasonable ways, again both within countries and between different countries and individuals or groups in different countries. And there are of course various ways, many of which have been discussed in this book, in which the West ought to play its part in helping to create a just and sustainable world society.

Nevertheless most people in Western countries do not care all that much about the longterm future of the environment or care much about the poverty of the Third World, *let alone* care much about *both* of these things in a combined way. Some of the obstacles to accepting the approach developed in this chapter will be faced in the next chapter. What however we have seen is that a combined approach is both possible and coherent, and that the phrase 'the just and sustainable society' provides an effective vehicle for its expression. [9]

Chapter 8

RESOURCE SCARCITY AND THE PROBLEMS OF GROWTH

An Argument

Given the fact that finiteness of natural resources imposes
an overall necessity for world consumption to be stabilised,
and given that there ought to be an increase in the use of
resources by developing countries in order to tackle
absolute poverty, it follows that the West ought to cut done
on its use of natural resources and give up policies of
economic growth.[1]

Such an argument will no doubt strike most readers as being
as dubious as it is bold. It is certaily bold and challenging, but, if the discussion of this chapter is on the right
lines, it is fairly near the truth. In any case it raises
a number of big issues which must be discussed if the
relationship between world poverty and the environment is to
be squarely faced. The variety of issues raised can be
better indicated if we attempt a more formal presentation of
the argument:

(1) The goal of a just and sustainable world society ought
    to be pursued
(2) We have already reached the limit in the use of natural
    resources if the goal of a sustainable world society
    is to be achieved
(3) Therefore there ought to be stabilisation in total world
    consumption of natural resources
(4) Global social justice requires that poor countries have
    an increase in their use of natural resources in order
    to reach reasonable living standards and then to sustain
    them
(5) A policy of stabilising the use of natural resources on
    a global scale entails that, if one part of the world
    has an increase in the use of natural resources, then
    another part must have a reduction
(6) Rich countries could reduce their use of natural
    resources and remain sustainable
(7) Therefore rich countries ought to accept a policy of
    reducing their use of natural resources
(8) Levels of economic activity are closely linked to the
    rate of use of natural resources
(9) Therefore, rich countries ought to reject a policy of

economic growth and accept a gradual reduction in levels of economic activity.

This argument *as an argument* is a sound one. If one accepts all the premisses (1,2,4,5,6) and the intermediate conclusions (3,7), then the final conclusion (9) certainly follows - at least if one accepts a further implicit premiss that if two moral imperatives (here (1) and (4)) *can* both be followed without contradiction, then a moral conclusion simply follows from the consequences of their combination.

No doubt however many readers will react to this argument with the thought: "There *must* be something wrong somewhere. Even if the argument is formally sound at least one of the premisses must be mistaken. For the conclusion is quite extraordinary and contrary to our intuitions". And indeed there is little doubt that each of the substantive premisses is liable to be rejected by one group of thinkers or another.

First, the *goal* of a just and sustainable world may be rejected as a moral goal from the outset. This might be because the whole idea of sustainability is rejected, or because the idea of a sustainable *world* is rejected and one is only interested in sustaining one's own society.

Second, one might be more of an optimist than environmentalists typically are and think that we are neither in a situation nor approaching a situation in which the world cannot sustain ever increasing exploitation of natural resources.

Third, one might reject the moral claim that social justice requires richer nations to change their ways in order that poverty may be alleviated in Third World countries: this position would involve a rejection of the idea of *international* obligations based on social justice.

Fourth, one might question whether a reduction in the use of resources by a richer country is really compatible with the sustaining of that country, on the grounds that such a reduction would imply economic decline and hence the end in any meaningful sense of a sustainable society.

Fifth, one might, on a rather different tack, take issue with the assumption that economic growth is dependent on using more resources, and hence claim that economic growth is quite compatible with a reduction in the use of natural resources.

Finally, one might overturn the argument as a whole by claiming that no country could possibly be obliged to accept a policy of no growth. This would be based partly on the recognition that no country *could* pursue such a policy, and partly on the recognition of a *third* moral principle that countries are *entitled* to pursue growth: this third moral principle comes into conflict with the consequences of the other two in the argument, and in the circumstances undermines the force of the argument.

What makes the argument interesting is the variety of ways in which one might reject it! Some of these are worth exploring further since they take us into substantial issues in moral and political philosophy. We shall claim that the first four objections above are unacceptable and that premisses (1), (2), (4) and (6) all stand. Nothing more will be said however about premiss (2), the *factual* premiss which forms the starting point of any environmental concern. This is taken as read: if the reader thinks it is quite false, he will find the remaining discussion of merely 'academic' interest. On the other hand, the rejection of sustainability, the rejection of Western obligation to the Third World and the rejection of the possibility of sustainability in the West at lower levels of resource usage will all receive critical attention. If we turn however to the last two objections, we will find that they have some validity. For it is indeed true that a country is entitled to the pursuit of growth: but as it is *also* true that growth is quite compatible with not increasing or with even reducing the rate of use of newly extracted natural resources, the pursuit of growth is quite consistent with the pursuit of global sustainability *and* the pursuit of Third World Development.

That then outlines the programme for the rest of this chapter. It is first worth noting however just how radical the argument is as it stands. For its main thrust is clearly directed against the standard view of the relationship between growth in developing countries and growth in Western countries. It is often argued by Western economists and politicians that Western countries can help poor countries best through the 'trickle-down' mechanism. A strong economy generates surplus wealth which can then be given in the form of Aid or transferred in the form of investments and loans in poor countries. It is also significant that those developmentalists who are very

97

critical of the Western record in helping poor countries, do not generally question the need for or justification of growth in Western countries. Rather they question the *kind* of growth involved and the *methods* used to pursue growth. They may claim that it is the fact that Western nations have tried to grow in competition with rather than in cooperation with poorer countries, which needs to be criticised, rather than the fact of growth itself. This seems incidentally to be one of the underlying themes of the Brandt report, which must be criticised for its assumption that unlimited growth in the use of material resources is possible.

What the above argument does then is to question the underlying assumption of both the conventional economist and the developmentalist critic of the conventional wisdom. This assumption is essentially that growth in developing countries can be combined with continued growth in Western nations so far as the foreseeable future is concerned. This assumption is challenged. It may have been possible up to now to combine growth in rich countries with growth in poor countries, and thus to say or think with a clear conscience "I am for growth in poor countries and I am for growth in rich countries". But now it is becoming increasingly difficult to accept the possibility of combined growth, and therefore difficult to avoid the following dilemma:

Either (i) "I am for continued affluence in the West and against significant growth in poorer countries", or (ii) "I am prepared to accept a reduction in material affluence in the West and I am for growth in developing countries". The dilemma is rarely perceived in this stark form, but its force will be increasingly felt as pressures on diminishing resources increase. And unless we are prepared to look at honestly and question our underlying commitment to affluence and the continued growth which it entails, that commitment will blur our perception of our moral obligation to help poor countries with the growth which it is far more important to achieve.

This argument is a profoundly disturbing one. For unless there is a transformation of attitudes argued for in this book, sometime in the foreseeable future pressure for resources from Western industrialised countries will erode their commitment (such as it presently is) to development in the Third World. This would no doubt be 'justified' in terms of national survival, and its consequence would probably be that the Third world will respond in such ways as to precipitate major global conflict or conflagration.

That such a development may occur is unfortunately a real possibility. But the fact that it occurred would not of course invalidate the argument that we ought not to have allowed it to happen. Moral arguments are not invalidated by moral failures. So whatever the future prospects, let us turn to the credentials of the argument itself. How might it be criticised?

It may be that a critic takes issue with the first premiss because he does not believe in moral commitments to *global* goals. He may accept that each country does - and ought to - pursue the goal of its own sustainability (and justice as well), but beyond this moral objectives are inappropriate and out of order. If that is the criticism, the issue concerns the propriety of global ethics, and the criticism represents a rejection of the approach of the whole book. Some comment on this issue will be made in the next section.

But a critic may rather base his objection on the claim that *sustainability* is not, as such, a proper object of moral commitment: some of us may be prudently concerned about our future or that of our children, but what happens in the future or what state a society will be in is not of present *moral* concern. This line of thought raises big issues discussed at greater length elsewhere.[2] Briefly, it is intuitively very odd not to think that a dimension to moral responsibility is a concern to preserve or promote what is valuable in one's society. A society which did not care whether it continued to exist or continued to flourish, would be in a de-moralised state and would have ceased to flourish already.

There is also the more formal point that, from a moral point of view, the *timing* of some state of affairs is in certain respects unimportant. A human being's flourishing, for instance, is a good thing, whether this occurs today, tomorrow or fifty years hence, and ought in principle to be promoted. In practice of course we give much more weight to the present; for the present, or to be more precise, the *near* future is much more in our control. But the idea that the future is a proper object of moral concern is surely to be granted.

Western Obligation: Myth or Reality?

The most serious criticism of the argument will come from those who question premiss (4) concerning the requirements of social justice, and question, in parallel, the global dimension to sustainability in premiss (1). The questioning may come from two sources. First, the claim may be made that it is *precisely* our present global crisis that *removes* any commitments we might have had before to the Third World or to global goals. Second, the objection may rest on a *general* view of international relations, according to which there are no Western obligations to the Third World anyway, or indeed to any 'common good' globally speaking. Let us look at the former line of thought first.

The argument is that the facts of the world today, especially those concerned with resource shortage, *undermine* the arguments given elsewhere in this book concerning our substantial obligation to help alleviate world poverty. This counter-attack may come from a self-styled environmentalist or conservationist who rejects the conclusion of the previous chapter. But it is as likely to come from any thinker - politician, businessman, shopsteward, housewife or academic - who sees himself or herself as a 'realist' and as avoiding the errors of moralism and idealism.

Consider the following three arguments, each of which starts with the same fundamental premise:

A1. There is a high probability that within the foreseeable future the international system of cooperation wil break down, either through global nuclear war or a dramatic increase in pressure for and fighting over scarce resources. Indeed the latter may be the trigger for the former.

A2. The obligation to help alleviate poverty is based upon the assumption that such assistance will secure development of some permanence: otherwise the money spent is like pouring water into a leaky bucket. But it is already clear that absolute poverty is not being reduced and the gap between rich and poor countries remains. The trends indicated under A1 mean that all gains in development will be wiped out in the chaos to come.

A3. Therefore: We are relieved of any substantial obligation to alleviate world poverty.

A second related argument might go as follows:

B1. As in A1.
B2. Patterns of international obligation and responsibility will simply cease to exist when the international 'community' has been destroyed and the world order has collapsed.
B3. But the sense of impending collapse is already collapse. That is, the situation of global breakdown already exists as a psychological reality.
B4. Therefore: International obligations *already* have little or no weight, and the West ceases to have a significant obligation to help alleviate poverty.

And a third argument might run as follows:

C1. As in A1.
C2. In a state of impending international breakdown, each nation or group has the right to pay a high degree of attention to its own survival and to prepare for the crisis of survival when it comes.
C3. Therefore: Nations are justified in looking to their own interests and ignoring the fate of other countries and of the absolute poor in other countries.[3]

These related arguments are not given here because a lot of space will be given to answering every point in them, but because they represent an ensemble of attitudes which are implicit if rarely articulated in full in the thinking of many people about our global situation. It is the general attitude of mind in which these arguments seem forceful which needs to be criticised. But first one or two specific comments on the arguments would be useful.

The first argument betrays two kinds of misunderstanding. First, the continuing gap between rich and poor countries is not an inevitable one. It could be reduced if we did more. So long as the channels of international co-operation are open, we ought to use them more, not less. But the second point is that even if the gap is not being reduced, the situation would be far worse if no assistance were given. The bucket analogy anaesthetises us from the realisation that it is real human beings whose lives are saved and whose crippling diseases are cured or prevented through programmes of assistance, even if the statistical patterns remain the same or depressingly similar.

The second argument again involves two errors. First, it grossly exaggerates the sense of impending crisis - a point to be taken up shortly. Second, it is only partly right in what it asserts in premiss B4. In the early chapters we found that there are two sources of obligation or moral demand. First there is the fundamental responsibility of agents to further the good or welfare of others, where they are in a position to do so, and second, there are the obligations which arise from membership of societies or communities, with general ties of reciprocity and specific ties of agreements to co-operate. Now it is clear that the general obligation to help others depends upon the capacity to help, and that this capacity to help would in the event of global collapse be largely non-existent, because the international economic and communications networks would have ceased to exist. But the obligation to assist others would still exist in principle: it would simply lack a context of application. And it certainly continues to have application in the world as it is and would do so right until the time when collapse really had set in.

On the other hand, the obligations which exist in virtue of our being members of international community or global society would indeed cease to exist, just because the relationships and institutions which embody that community or society would have ceased to exist. But the corollary to this is that we should affirm our obligations under international institutions, when they are under threat, not abandon them on the first pretext.[4] The same points need to be made about the third argument: but criticism of the 'right to pursue self-interest' argument will come later on.

But it may be felt that the main issue really rests with the first premiss. Are things really as bad as it makes out? Are we really already in a situation where the sense of impending doom makes us already, in psychological terms, geared to an attitude of breakdown? This is partly of course a matter of factual assessment. And I would argue that the 'facts' are not as bad as all that. But it is also a matter of basic attitudes, as we shall see. First, there are two points to be made about the 'facts'.

It is difficult to estimate how probable global breakdown is. No-one really knows. But what is reasonably certain is that its probability is partly a product of the attitudes

and reactions of human beings to the possibility of its
occurrence. If nations now adopt the siege mentality, if
they give up helping poor countries, if they continue to
arm and engage in deterrence whatever the cost, if they are
determined to maintain material standards by belligerent
competition for scarce resources, then the probability of
the scenario outlined above is *much more likely* to come
about than if nations did not do such things. On the premise
that no nation stands to gain from global breakdown, it
would seem to follow that the rational thing for nations to
do is to reduce the probability of this happening, by
putting more effort into international co-operation,
development programmes, disarmament efforts, global conservation measures, and so on, rather than less.

However this line of thought would not convince someone of
a 'doomsday' persuasion who thought that global collapse
was either inevitable or highly probable. He would reason
that there is little or nothing that nations can do to avert
it, and so the sensible thing to do is for nations to forget
about the rest of the world and prepare as best they can
for the worst. Such a policy would also be morally justified
since the world is already, in psychological terms, fragmented, and the necessary basis for international obligations
has already gone.

The answer to this is that even if the probability is high
that global collapse will come some time in the foreseeable
future, that prospect does not mean that the present state
of the world is one on the verge of collapse or one that
one can with justification treat as 'about-to-collapse'.
Far from it. Whatever the dangers, the present reality in
the world is one of a highly connected and co-operative
whole. We are not to be sure a very united world. But the
vast machinery of the United Nations system along with many
other international organisations clearly bears witness to
the great extent to which we are a deeply interconnected and
inter-dependent world. We are far from being a world
fragmented into many isolated parts. But again it must be
granted that if a person's perception of the world and its
future is really so doom-laden that it already presents
itself as 'fragmented', then these arguments will carry no
weight. For appeals to the reality of interconnectedness
or of world community or of the real possibilities of
development, will seem like so much talk, so much paper-thin

delusion to cover up the real cracks that are already there and spreading.

The Moral Basis of Optimism

Is then the difference between us basically one of differing estimates of probabilities? Is it that whereas I recognise the genuine possibility of collapse and the real chance of averting it through collective action, my opponent sees it as a high probability with little chance of averting it? This may be part of the difference, but it is not the important difference. We get nearer the truth if we say that I am an optimist and he is a pessimist. Now the chief difference between optimism and pessimism is one of attitude not one of factual assessment. An optimist and a pessimist might agree that a pint bottle has half a pint of water in it, but one will say it is half full, the other it is half empty. But we need to say more about this difference of approach. For optimism here is a basic attitude of mind; it involves an active commitment to work for the good that is possible, a sense of moral commitment and a sense of morale or strength in attempting it.[5] Pessimism here involves a passive despairing, a retreat from moral commitment into apathy or self-interest, and a loss of morale or willingness to take bold steps.

The central feature here is the strong sense of moral commitment. For this is not so much the *consequence* of the optimistic attitude as its *ground*. Conversely it is the lack of a sense of moral commitment to international obligations which is perhaps the chief cause of the pessimistic reaction to the crisis and dangers which affect the world. It may be recalled that the basic argument to which we have been objecting is one to the effect that the real possibility of global collapse *undermined* our international obligations, and in particular our obligation to assist in development in poor countries. The truth, it may be observed, is rather the other way round. It is only *if* one is not already fully committed to the idea of international morality, that one is liable to be drawn into the attitude of deep pessimism, i.e. pulled into the psychological frame of mind that sees the world as already fragmented and international obligations as will o' the wisps. This basic point no doubt oversimplifies, but it contains a basic truth.

104

A serious commitment to internationalism, support for international institutions and acceptance of the deep links between ourselves and peoples of other countries, are not based on intellectual assessment alone, but on a whole way or perceiving and feeling about the world. This sense of internationalism is such that one's response to the possibility of global catastrophe and of development efforts coming to nothing, is not to despair, but to search for international solutions and to work for development whatever the risks.

The arguments of doomsday pessimists then do not show that we *no longer* have international obligations towards the poor of the world. Rather they reveal that their advocates never really accepted the obligations anyway. The argument from the probabilities of global breakdown is a kind of cover-up, albeit unintentional, for not accepting, not really accepting, the moral arguments all along.

The Rejection of International Obligations

Still, it may be insisted, may there not be something in not accepting the moral arguments all along? It is not obvious that morality has to have an international or global dimension. We all learn what morality is through its existence in the society or community in which we are born and brought up, but it is not clear that its domain extends beyond each separate cultural sphere. The answer to this argument lies essentially in the general drift of this book, but perhaps a reminder of several points is in order at this point.

The rejection of the general idea that countries, groups or individuals within countries have moral obligations towards other countries, groups or individuals therein, rests on one of two approaches, which are actually significantly different from one another. First, it may be said that there is no such thing as international morality. For there is no point of view beyond a particular society's morality which could represent the global or international perspective. There are many particular moralities, but no one universal morality.[6]

This point however is both irrelevant and fake. First, it is irrelevant because there is no reason at all why the dominant morality of a given society should not contain - and indeed many such moralities do contain - universal prescriptions concerning the conduct of individuals, groups or states in relation to all other individuals, groups or states. Indeed the fundamental principle concerning helping others in need is derived from a version of Christian morality within Western societies, but it is intended to be applied in principle to anyone in need in whatever society. It does not depend upon that person's being in one's society or even sharing one's moral standards.

But the claim that there is no international point of view from which to derive an international morality is factually mistaken as well. For any candid look at the workings of international institutions, at the establishment of international conventions and covenants, or at the vast area of economic transactions, shows quite clearly the existence of international morality. Indeed if one did not know of its existence, one would be bound to assume it, for all the ingredients within a society which make morality necessary and natural are also present in the international sphere - inter-dependence, the need for agreements, goals pursued effectively only through collaboration, rules for the peaceful settlement of conflicts of interest, and so on. To be sure there is much debate about what the principles of international ethics should be. But the fact that thinkers dispute over the content of international ethics should no more cast doubt on the reality of international morality, than does the fact that there are disagreements about morality within ordinary societies cast doubt on the reality of those moralities.

The other argument which is sometimes used to discount any international obligations is rather different. It does not deny that there is such a thing as an international moral perspective. Rather it claims that if you adopt it, all you get is the recognition that each country has the *right* to pursue its own interests, not that some countries have an obligation to help others to pursue their interests, like the alleviation of poverty within a poor country.[7]

The difficulty with this argument is that if the right is supposed to be absolute or unrestricted, the doctrine rapidly becomes incoherent. For if every country has the right to pursue its interests in whatever way it pleases, then it is justified whatever it does, and no other country, whatever its treatment from that country, has any grounds for complaint. If one country invades another, forcefully exploits its resources and so on, it has a right to do so given that it regards these courses of action as in its interests. And of course the other country has the right to hit back if it is powerful enough to do so.

Now the unrestrainted pursuit of power, checked only by the similar pursuits of other powerful countries no doubt matches many actual historical cases, and has also been given a moral veneer with the claim that 'might is right'.[8] Nevertheless, the line of thought hardly represents a proper *moral* argument. For all it does is to *legitimise* whatever actually happens in the interaction of states pursuing their interests, by implying that there is no moral point of view from which to *criticise* what states have done, or to exercise a *normative* influence upon what states may propose to do. And if that is what our opponent really wants to say, namely that states do pursue their interests and there is no international standpoint from which to criticise what they do, then we are not really dealing with an international morality. For its existence is being effectively denied. And that argument has already been dealt with.

If on the other hand one recognises that the 'right' of nations to pursue their interests is not an absolute one, then a different and more acceptable account can be given, but not one that helps our critic in the present issue. It makes little sense to say that a country has a right to something unless one also says that other countries have an obligation to respect that right. Thus the right not to be attacked or the right to autonomy are paralleled by the obligation of other countries not to attack it or interfere with the internal decision-making of that country. Correspondingly that country has an obligation to respect the same rights that other countries have.

So if the phrase 'the right to pursue national interests' is to have a genuinely moral content, then it must be interpreted in the following way. (i) It is shorthand for saying that there are certain more specific rights, like the right not to be attacked, which each country has, and corresponding to these rights are obligations on the part of each country to respect these rights in other countries.

107

But we must note, of course, that countries do not just have rights, they have obligations as well, and we now have a system of international obligations - which is what our critic did not wish to accept. (ii) The second thing suggested by the phrase 'right to pursue its own interests' is that within the constraints of a country's obligations in the international sphere, e.g. in respecting other country's rights or in pursuing the reduction of poverty, a country, like an individual, has the liberty to pursue its interest as it thinks fit. That is, from the point of view of other nations, a country has a 'moral space' or morally neutral area of choice analogous to that of individuals discussed in chapter 2. But note again that this right exists against a background of obligations. So talk of rights, at least in any moral context, necessarily brings us back to a wider moral theory of an international kind. It is worth remarking in passing that if the view that countries have the right to pursue their own interests is inspired by the rather selfish consideration concerning the right to keep or control one's resources, then there is a rather curious backlash to it. For the record of Western nations in regard to the use of other countries' resources leaves much to be desired.

The above argument does not amount to showing that Western nations have the specific obligation to help alleviate world poverty. It simply establishes that nations do have international obligations. That the obligation to alleviate poverty is amongst those obligations needs further argument, which will be found in other parts of the book. Suffice it to say here that if one accepts that individuals have a right to the necessities of life, then national governments in other countries no less than individuals in other countries share in the obligation to provide those necessities. The right then of a developing country to receive development assistance and the obligation of richer nations to provide it can be seen as deriving from the collective right of many individuals to receive the necessities of life.

Growth

If we return to the main argument set out at the beginning of the chapter, we can see how some of the main objections to it fail. But we now need to turn to the other objections which turn on the supposed connection between use of material

resources and growth and on the commitment to growth.
These can be discussed together. We can approach these
issues by examining the claim that the argument is in a
sense quite unrealistic. That is, there is something
quite unrealistic about the conclusion that the West ought
to give up a policy of growth. However theoretically
correct the argument may look, it just could not be acted
on.

People who perceive their economic situation as one not of
growth but of stagnation or decline, would not regard this
as desirable or something which they might make an object
of pursuit, whether for reasons of morality or for reasons
of longterm self-interest. For in such a situation, people
would either be demoralised or deadened by the sense of
decline, or be resilient enough to fight what they say as
decline and return to a state of growth. Either way they
would not advocate or actively pursue a policy of no growth
or the reverse of growth.

This verdict, if correct, is a rather devastating one, and
threatens to undermine the emphasis upon the moral commitment
to development which runs through this book. For if 'ought'
implies 'can', and it is shown that generally speaking
people *cannot* do otherwise than aim for growth, any 'ought'
based on the need for us to accept no growth is quite unreal
and insubstantial. In other words, the argument in this
paragraph seeks either to undermine premiss (6) in the main
argument, or to challenge the conclusion directly by claiming that countries have the right or entitlement to pursue
growth. For it suggests that Western countries *do* need to
continue to grow if they are to remain vital and dynamic
societies, or societies which are worth sustaining. Indeed
the real thrust of this line of thought is that societies
are *entitled* to pursue growth, that they could not be
expected to do otherwise. So if the earlier argument
really does point to the 'either or' dilemma given earlier,
so much the worse for our obligation to poor countries. It
becomes diminished or destroyed.

This argument brings us back to the 'anticipation of global
collapse' argument criticised earlier. But the objection
to it here will be of a rather different kind. For what
needs to be challenged is the assumption which is made in
all the arguments and counter-arguments which have been

considered so far in this chapter. It is the assumption that growth or development entails a continued increase in the use of material resources. In the original argument it is premiss (8) which is the key premise upon which we should focus our critical attention. There are two quite distinct ways in which we can deny the equivalence of growth with increasing use of resources.

First, even if growth or development is thought of primarily in terms of the generally increasing availability of material products which contribute to safety, comfort, convenience and various essential services, it must not be assumed that this increase must be paralleled by an increase in the use of *newly extracted* resources. For the development of new technologies and their products, or energy conservation systems, of increased re-cycling of material resources may all mean that growth in material standards of living is not paralleled by growth in new resource usage, and may even be accompanied by a reduced level of such usage. It is therefore quite possible for a society to be committed to growth but at the same time committed to reducing its usage of new natural resources. Whether and how far Western societies *will* do this remains to be seen. But it is possible.

Second, growth or development should not be thought of simply in terms of the availability of valued material products. Ultimately growth or development should be seen in terms of human beings flourishing, and achieving happiness through the development of their capacities and meaningful relationships with others. A society can be said to show growth in this sense, when more and more of its members achieve a state of flourishing, happiness or well-being. But growth here is not simply an increase in the number of individuals flourishing *in* a society; it is also a growth of social networks, patterns and relationships which partly constitute that society and which facilitate the flourishing of individuals.

Growth then in this sense is measured in terms of human flourishing, not in terms of the use of or possession of material products. Up to a certain point there is a close connexion between the two. The various elements of human flourishing such as stable human relationships, participation in a rich and diverse culture and in the life of one's community, the development and exercise of capacities,

110

interesting past-times and so on, all depend to some extent upon the existence of adequate material products, both for the individual and in the society at large. One needs adequate food, shelter, warmth, tools, gadgets and a vast range of other artefacts not just for survival, but for pleasure and convenient forms of living. But it is only up to a certain point that there is a close connection or causal dependence. Beyond that point there ceases to be much connection. Growth in material standards or the use of or possession of material objects may not be accompanied by growth in the quality of living: indeed the former may be an impediment to the latter if the desire for it becomes a preoccupation. Conversely growth in the quality of living in the individual or in the community as a whole need not be accompanied by a corresponding growth in the use of material products.

In Western societies the levels of affluence experienced by many people are far in excess of what is generally necessary for human flourishing.[9] On the other hand, there is plenty of scope for growth in the things that make for human flourishing. It is therefore quite possible to be committed to growth, i.e. growth in the things that matter, whilst being prepared to go for 'no growth' in the more conventional sense. And there need be no sense of demoral- isation about valuing one's society in these terms. Quite the reverse. It is perhaps a sad irony that within Western societies many of those who are very affluent do not really flourish because their desire to retain their affluence breeds deep anxieties over its retention, whilst those who envy this affluence see this affluence as the key to their own flourishing when all the time they really have quite enough themselves to be flourishing.

On the other hand it seems clear that in developing countries the vast majority of people live below, in many cases well below, the level of material well-being necessary for human flourishing, and though some aspects of what is valuable in human life such as family love and sense of community may survive the most appalling conditions, there is little doubt that the quality of life is critically related to the use and availability of material products and artefacts. There is perhaps a rough analogy betwen growth in a society and growth in an individual. What is most striking about growth in the early stages of an individual's life is physical growth, but beyond a certain point it is mental powers that go on growing. So likewise what is important about a society below a certain level of material well-being is that its growth is marked by an increase in its use of material resources. But beyond a certain level of affluence, what is important is the continuing growth of cultural vitality, richness and so on. So long as it is free of any evaluative overtones about being grown-up or not, the analogy may be useful for making the point that increase in the use of material resources is important in developing countries in a way it is not in the richer countries of the West.

The upshot of the preceding discussion is as follows. Growth has much less to do with increasing the use of natural resources than is usually assumed. The recognition of this can come partly from accepting greater efficiency or extraction of value in the use of resources, and partly from accepting that beyond a certain level of material well-being non-material sources of self-fulfilment take on proportionally greater importance. A society which has lost its sense of growth or development is indeed in trouble, for it would be like food which has lost its savour. No moral argument could possibly have as its conclusion the demand that a society should cease to grow or lose its sense of growth. For a society's deepest imperative is that it should continue to flourish or grow to greater flourishing. On the other hand, if growth is not tantamount to the increasing use of the world's limited resources, there is no reason why all countries, rich or poor, should not grow, and there is no reason why the moral obligation on rich countries to help poor countries should not have full application, even against the backcloth of future resource limitations. For our growth, as here interpreted, is quite consistent with allowing and indeed facilitating development in poorer countries, where *their* development may indeed involve the increased use of resources.

This then represents the general verdict of this chapter. Before we conclude however, a further difficulty needs to be faced. The reader may have the following kind of thought:

All right, suppose that people in Western societies do generally come to see growth as you have depicted, do commit themselves to greater efficiency in resource usage, and do perceive that growth in human well-being is possible in a situation of non-growth in the usage of resources. Then no doubt what you say follows and the obligation to assist poor countries can be acknowledged, since the sense of growth which is important to people is not given up. But suppose, *as is more likely to be the case,* that the vast majority of people do not see growth in this way, and believe that growth and affluence are tied to the ever increasing use of natural resources. What then? Surely you cannot expect them to acknowledge any significant obligation, if they see the well-being of their own society as being, or becoming, incompatible with helping poor countries? Surely this obligation does not exist, given what *they* believe about growth.

What reply is to be made to this? The second supposition is sadly a very real one and probability is on its side. It may very well come about that pressure on resources, applied in the name of growth as conventionally understood, will blind rich nations to their obligations to the Third World and in the international sphere generally. But one must take issue with the last assumption. The obligation exists, whether we recognise it or not. For the obligation rests not on what people think their situation is, but upon what it really is. Given a proper understanding of what growth is and of what is essential to the flourishing of a society and its members, it is clear that the facts about resources do not render the obligation to assist poor countries null and void. If people do not have this understanding, then they *ought* to have it. Objective moral arguments - especially on complex social issues - often depend upon facts which those to whom the argument is directed do not, or do not yet, accept. So part of the business of persuasion is to get them to accept the facts as well as the moral conclusion. I could be wrong about growth, as about many things in this book, and there is no escaping the fact that any complex moral thesis gives hostages to factual fortune. So it is up to the reader to assess the fortunes of my facts.

In the last two chapters we have envisaged the scenario of increasing pressure on natural resources, and it has been argued that even in this case our obligation to help poor countries is not suspended, but must be integrated into environmentalist programmes of change. It may of course be that things are not as gloomy as we have supposed. New resources may be found, new energy sources may be found and so on. I should be glad if it turns out so. But of course in that case no doubts can be raised about our obligations to the poor of the world. However in our present world situation, it would be a foolish developmentalist who thought that we need not bother about putting the brakes on material comsumption in the West. Concern for justice now must not blind us to the real problems of sustainability which lie in front of us.

Chapter 9

ARMAMENTS, VIOLENCE AND WORLD POVERTY

Several issues arise when one seeks to relate world poverty
to such factors as the Arms Race and violence. First, there
is the evident fact that vast sums of money are spent on the
Super-powers Arms Race and more generally by all countries
throughout the world. What are the implications of this,
in the light such statements as that made in the Brandt
Report that "The annual military bill is now approaching
450 billion US dollars, while official development aid
accounts for less than 5 per cent of that figure"?[1] Second,
the discussion will centre on the nature of violence and its
connection to world poverty.

'The Arms Race Kills'

There is a Quaker poster based on a statement by Philip
Noel-Baker which simply says 'The Arms Race is killing'.[2]
(This will be adapted to 'The Arms Race Kills' for the
purposes of discussion here.) It is no doubt an overstatement intended to make one think, but what is interesting is
whether it is a helpful or misleading overstatement. That
it is an overstatement, in the sense of using language beyond
its normal idiomatic context, seems undeniable. The basis
of the judgment is of course the view that much of the money
spend on defence, on arms and military training, could be
and probably would be spent on Third World Development, if
it were not spent on the Arms Race or more generally on
military spending by all governments and other armed groups.
If that money were spent on Third World development, many
people who do die would not have died, and many people who
do lead physically and mentally maimed, stunted or degrading
lives would through escaping from absolute poverty not be
leading maimed, stunted or degrading lives. So one could
say, by a natural extention, 'The Arms Race kills, maims,
stunts and degrades' or, even more generally, 'military
spending kills, maims, stunts and degrades'.

But of course these formulations, wider as they are, contain
exactly the same overstatement. For the Arms Race or
military spending or, to be more precise, those engaged in
them do not *literally* kill, maim, stunt or degrade the poor
of the world. No bullet need be fired, no bomb need be
exploded, no action need be performed which has as its

intention that people be dead or maimed. There is thus an
immense difference between failing to spend money on preventing deaths because you are spending it on something else
like arms, education or pleasure, and acting with the
intention that someone should be killed or die. Failures of
the former kind do not normally attract the active verbs such
as 'kill' or 'maim'.

Statements like 'the Arms Race Kills' nevertheless say
something important. What is it? Is it simply to remind us
that part of what is spent on armaments *could be* spent on the
eminently desirable objective of reducing world poverty?
This cannot be all that is meant. Suppose I said that
'Government spending on education kills'. It is undoubtedly
true that part of the money spent on education *could be*
spent on world development. But it is doubtful whether
anyone would find it in the least helpful to say such a
thing. Why? Because that judgment contains a *moral* judgment
to the effect that we ought not spend so much on education
and that the money saved ought to be spent on development.
And no one would make that judgment. But this shows us what
the true colours of the original statement are. What
attracts some people to the judgment 'the Arms Race Kills'
and what gives others a gut reaction of antipathy towards it,
is precisely the implicit moral judgment it contains, namely:
Less ought to be spent on the Arms Race, and (part of) the
money saved ought to be devoted to development.

This gives us the *force* of the judgment which is often
intended (there is also something else which may be meant,
mentioned later). It amounts to a moral assertion. Or
rather it amounts to a double assertion: (a) Less ought to
be spent on the Arms race; (b) (part of) the money saved ough
to be spent on development. They are both necessary. For
someone who thought that we ought to continue with high
defence spending but that we ought to give more for development by increasing Aid from *other* budget allocations or
through greater private giving, would not accept that the
arms race kills - though he might think that 'government
apathy and private affluence kill'. And someone who thought
that there ought to be a reduction in arms spending but that
the money saved should be devoted to, say, more education
here and not to overseas aid, would again not accept the
proposition 'the Arms Race Kills' - though he might think
that 'the Arms Race curtails knowledge'. (People would

probably not speak like this, but the logic of their positions would be similar.)

If one is then to argue for the spirit of this judgment, one must defend both propositions. Now there are two levels on which the argument can proceed. On the lower level, one tackles the issue as one of relative priorities. One accepts that Governments operate within budgetary constraints and the issue is over how much of the public money available is to be spent on different objectives, such as defence, education, housing, health care, Aid, local government, police, sport, the arts and so on. One would then argue that the relative weighting of all these things is in certain respects *wrong*. One would argue first of all that the Government does not give enough weight to its obligations towards the Third World. One would then argue that one area at least where the money might come from would be defence. There might be plenty of other reasons for arguing for a defence cut, but one reason would be that the money saved *would* go towards the fulfilling of our obligation to the Third World.

At this level then it is a question of arguing over relative priorities. The force of the argument will partly depend upon the strength of the positive arguments for our obligation to help alleviate world poverty - and on this issue nothing more needs to be added here. (With regard to the other part of the argument, there are all sorts of reasons some of which are indicated briefly later.) How powerful is the argument by itself that the money saved from defence *would* help with development? At a theoretical level it certainly gives a genuine reason for reducing defence expenditure. However it is doubtful whether at a practical level it can exercise an effective leverage in persuading other of orthodox political or military thinking. Why is this?

If a person has the standard sort of perception of defence issues and is fully committed to the 'imperatives of defence', then he is unlikely to be swayed by the consideration of what would be achieved with money saved for morally laudable goals such as world development, or for that matter other socially desirable objectives within his own country. He will tend to see all these concerns, including the concern for world poverty, as jostling for priority in the budgetary pecking order *after* the vital commitments to defence are made. If on the other hand, he comes to question the whole standard approach to defence issues, to the logic of deterrence and so on, then he would not need the separate argument about what would be achieved for development in order to see the propriety of cuts in defence spending.

This leads us to the second higher level of argument. For the issue is not really just one of an exercise in relative weightings. It is really about achieving a major shift in political thinking. A major reduction in military spending is not going to come about through trying to press the obligation to the Third world, or the obligation to keep our social services going for that matter. It will only come about if there is a significant shift away from the militaristic mentality, and associated with it the attitudes of national security. A greater sense of international identity is crucial, not only because it will slacken the grip which the imperatives of defence have upon countries, but also because it would make people see more clearly the nature of international commitments and the clear global imperative which world poverty presents us with. The standard commitment to defence is not in reality just one consideration amongst others; it is a goliath that tends to dominate and distort the whole system of priorities, and blurs our perception of international obligations. The ability to recognise the seriousness of our obligations to the world community and the ability to recognise that military logic is not the proper logic of national security and progress in the world, are really two sides of the same coin, two facets of the internationalism which is needed but desperately difficult to achieve.

It may be felt that too much has been made of the *moral* character of the claim that the Arms Race kills. And there is certainly another way in which it could be taken which makes it look like a *factual* claim. This claim would be that the Arms Race *causes* people to die. This is based not on the mere supposition that the money spent on the Arms Race *could have* been spent on preventing people from dying, but rather that it *would have* been so spent. Now there is undoubtedly something in this idea. And insofar as it is true, it usefully underlines the *tragedy* of military spending, that but for our commitment to armaments we *would* do a lot more about world poverty, and no doubt many other

118

socially desirable goals. It is probably true that many of those in positions of political power would certainly favour increasing Aid to developing countries, if only they did not think it imperative to use such vast sums of public money on defence.

If however we take it as a factual claim we must ask: *who* would wish to make such a claim? No doubt the factual claim is based on the view that those in power *would* give less *moral* priority to defence and more *moral* priority to development. Now either one approves of such changes in moral priority - because they are in line with one's own moral views - or one does not. It is surely obvious that if one did not approve, one would hardly go round saying 'the Arms Race Kills', even if one admitted that cuts in defence spending *would* result in greater development efforts. For the factual claim suggests, even if it does not strictly entail, certain moral assumptions which one rejects. Conversely, someone who does present it as a factual claim really has certain moral assumptions at the back of his mind. That is why he finds it useful to say it.

So the force of 'the Arms Race Kills' cannot lie mainly in the supposition of what would happen. It is what 'ought' to be done that gives it its punch. This may be illustrated with a different example. Suppose one meets a man who spends lots of money on winter sports and one suggests that some of the money might be spent on saving people's lives and (heaven forbid that one use such language) that 'his excessive love of winter sports kills people'. He might very well turn round and tell one that if he did not spend all his money on winter sports, he certainly *would not* spend it on saving people's lives, but rather on a hi-fi system or a sports car. We would not feel that because of this, 'his excessive love of winter sports kills people' had lost significance (assuming that we allowed this way of talking in the first place). For the implicit judgment that he ought not to spend so much on himself and that he ought to concern himself with, amongst other things, world poverty, is not affected by his lack of will. So likewise the force of 'The Arms Race Kills' does not depend upon its being true that the saving of lives *would* be the consequence of cuts in arms expenditure.

This discussion of the saying 'The Arms Race Kills' has

119

helped to bring out some of the complexities of the issues. There is little doubt that the causal and moral connections between arms expenditure and development are highly signif- icant and deserve to be given increased attention.[3] But it is important not to forget that if We in the West do not do as much as we ought to help alleviate world poverty, there are a variety of causes of it. It is not just the arms race, or the attitudes which make the imperatives of defence so powerful and appealing, which blind people to their oblig- ations or make those obligations have an undue lowness of priority. Many other things contribute to this process, ranging from specific weaknesses and prejudices to general indifference. Perhaps it is significant to say 'Indifference kills'. It is certainly interesting to note that Willy Brandt, in the introduction to the Brandt Report, says in the context of the arms spending - development connection, "Morally it makes no difference whether a human being is killed in war or is condemned to starve to death because of the indifference of others".[4]

Reasons for Disarmament

The present discussion would not be complete if something more was not said in defence of the claim that there ought to be a decrease in defence spending.[5] Clearly one moral basis for the claim would be pacifism, and some of the arguments which would be used by Quakers to defend the saying discussed earlier would be pacifist arguments. But one does not have to be a pacifist to have profound moral objections to high military spending in general and to nuclear arms in particular. One may object both to the wrong attitudes and priorities of value which underlie armament policies, and to the character and manner of employment of armaments. In particular, it is doubtful if nuclear weapons can legitimately be used or threatened as instruments of policy. On the traditional doctrine of the 'just war', for instance, nuclear weapons may be condemned on the grounds of being indiscriminate in effect, and, if aimed at centres of civilian population, on the grounds of being directed at non-combatants.[6]

But even if one is not convinced of the moral arguments, one should recognise powerful pragmatic arguments which show that it is not in our interests to remain locked into the arms race: and if it is not in a country's interests to pursue the arms race, then a government has a duty - a moral duty to its citizens - to change its policy on armaments so that national interests are properly served. There is little doubt that the nuclear arms race is getting dangerously out of control, with new technological developments constantly adding further factors of instability. The dangers of accidental war remain. But, worse than that, the danger of nuclear war being deliberately started by a 'first strike' is becoming greater. Whether the idea of a 'winnable nuclear war' is an illusion or not, the fact that strategists are thinking in this way can only increase the probability of its occurring.

There is no safety in increasing armaments, and the world is poorer not safer because of the arms race. A safer policy lies in a concerted effort to bring about general disarmament. A useful start to this would be unilateral disarmament for Britain, since its independent deterrent is of no real significance at all. No doubt there are risks involved in disarmament, particularly in unilateral initiatives designed to break deadlocks. But the risks in disarmament are, to quote President Eisenhower, "as nothing compared with the risks of *not* disarming".[7]

What is perhaps most disturbing is the kinds of attitude which lie behind vast expenditures on arms. These are justified in the name of national security: but there is limited vision of what security might involve, and of how far greater security could be achieved through greater forms of international cooperation and support for the U.N. system, through bridge-building and the reduction of fear and mistrust. The propaganda war paints the world in black and white, and we fail to see that it is nearly all shades of grey. It portrays countries as either aggressive or defensive, and we fail to see that most countries, including the super-powers, are both aggressive and defensive in public posture and private attitude. It is oversimple to say that nations ought not to defend themselves, but the fact remains that the general attitudes of peoples and governments towards internationalism are inadequate, and the commitment - often unquestioned - to massive defence spending is simply a reflection of those inadequate attitudes.

The facts about the arms race and general arms expenditure are appalling, they are tragic and they betoken, to anyone who can adopt an international vantage point, simply *collective madness.* But all these predicates - appalling, tragic, mad - which we all know in our heart to apply to this world, are stopped dead in their tracks by the 'Ah but ...' of the prudence and of the morality which are the products of our nationalistic identities. Thus prudence, seen through the standard perception of national self-interest, demands the logic of defence, and moral reasoning, understood in terms of the obligation of governments to promote that national interest, supports the demands of prudence.

Such a perspective is then not a fertile soil in which the sense of obligation towards the poor of the world can grow strong. Whilst there may be *some* improvement in Western governmental policy towards the Third World without a weakening of this nationalistic perspective, no *substantial* change is likely without it. Only a wider internationally oriented conception of prudence and morality can break the vice-like grip of the logic of defence, and give proper weight to the concerns for world poverty and other global concerns.

The steps towards this internationalist perspective are difficult to take. We need the attitude of trust and courage rather than that of caution, the attitude of optimism rather than that of pessimism. No doubt it requires, in the broadest sense, an act of faith. But this would at least enable us to see the utter incongruity of making a mad and tragic world with the assurance that this is a wise and morally justified thing to do.

Violence

Those who support the spirit of sayings like 'The Arms Race Kills' often quote the saying of President Eisenhower:
> Every gun that is made, every warship launched, every rocket fired, signifies in a final sense a *theft* from those who hunger and are not fed, from those who are cold and are not clothed. [8]

Again this saying contains, by conventional standards, the same kind of overstatement as the former saying. Yet it brings out important points. First, money which could be, or would be, spent on feeding and clothing people is *taken away* from these activities and given to armaments. Second, the poor have a *right* to these things - a right to the basic

necessities of life based on social justice - so that, in
some 'final' moral sense, taking away what they have a
right to constitutes a form of theft. Third, as the notion
of 'theft' suggests, armaments indirectly *make* the poor
remain poor or force them to remain in poverty, and hence
a kind of 'violence' or violation of basic rights' involved.

Of course those wedded to 'literal' meaning (which often
means that they are wedded to a cause, whether they realise
it or not) will protest. Money spent on arms is not taken
away from the poor: they did not have it in the first place,
nor was it first allocated to development and then stopped.
Theft cannot occur unless a person already possesses something according to the rules of property. Violence is
essentially an active and deliberate inflicting of suffering
or death, and the suggestion that we are doing violence to
people because we prefer to spend our money on arms rather
than development is a patently unwarranted distortion to
the meaning of 'violence'.

There is something in this protest. Nevertheless, one's
reactions to such overstatements reveals one's basic
values. If one *dismisses* them as nonsense because they
distort meaning, one implicitly rejects the moral evaluation
in them. If one welcomes them, even if they contain
hyperbole, then one accepts the moral evaluation in them,
namely that the poor do have a right to the basic necessities
of life, that we ought to do more to assist in development
and that our preoccupation with armaments either blurs our
perceptions or distorts our sense of priorities.

However sayings of the kind we have considered are not
merely 'quotable' hyperbolic devices for pointing to our
obligations to the poor of the world. They form part of
a rather different understanding of human relationships and
of moral responsibility from that of those who reject such
sayings. For part of what is at issue here is the scope of
moral responsibility which we discussed earlier. Are we
primarily responsible for what we directly aim at in our
actions? Or are we significantly responsible for the
unwanted but foreseeable *consequences* of what we do and of
our active policies? Are we also responsible for the
consequences of our omissions and patterns of non-involvement?

One of the most controversial and significant of concepts
in this area is that of violence itself. 'Violence' is an

exceedingly complex and confusing concept and the following remarks do not more than scratch the surface. What has stimulated interest in this concept at a theoretical level has been the supposed contrast between the 'radical' conceptions of 'structural', 'systemic' or 'institutional' violence, and the 'conventional' conception of violence. Yet it becomes clear that there is no 'one' radical conception nor 'one' conventional conception, but a range of overlapping accounts.

What then first comes to mind when we think of violence? We tend to visualise conspicuously violent acts of killing, assaulting or hitting. John Harris in *Violence and Responsibility* calls this usefully the 'rape, murder, fire sword paradigm'.[9] No doubt when we think of such acts we first think of terrorists or hooligans doing them. But reflection quickly reveals that, if we are after a basic *description* of what a violent act is, such a paradigm will fit the similar acts of soldiers. Violence then is not restricted, as is sometimes suggested, to something essential irrational, nor is it restricted only to those acts of which we happen strongly to disapprove. If killing someone with a gun is an act of violence, it is so whether a criminal does it, a terrorist does it or a member of the armed forces does it. The term 'violence' *can* of course be used restrictively for only those cases of killing or maiming which one wishes to condemn, and refused application in those cases which one regards as 'justified killing'. Undoubtedly one's moral evaluations do influence the range of things one is prepared to call 'violence'; nevertheless it seems unhelpful, and in a way dishonest, not to accept a basic descriptive core to violence. Whether fighting in a war is justified or not, surely there is no gainsaying that war is violent and partly made up of many deliberate acts of violence.

Violence, however, cannot be restricted to these 'paradigm' cases. First, violence is not simply manifested in *acts* of violence; it is also manifested in whole policies or pursuits of objectives. Few would dispute that a general is engaged in violence if his soldiers commit acts of violence on his orders, even if he does not fight himself. So too, by a natural extension, are members of a government who pursue a war objective.

Second, acts of violence do not necessarily involve *violent* acts. If one poisons a water supply so as to kill certain people, one's act is an act of violence, even if the activity of poisoning is as calm and unagitated as may be. Reflection on cases like this leads Harris to postulate a rather more general definition:

An act of violence occurs when injury or suffering is inflicted upon a person or persons by an agent who knows (or ought reasonably to have known), that his actions would result in the harm in question.[10]

Third, few people would deny that we should include under the harm that violence may cause *mental* suffering and damage as well. Parents and teachers, for instance, can be violent towards children without there being any physical violence at all. As one member of the Quaker Peace Action Caravan once put it:

To do violence to a person is to destroy, damage, diminish or degrade that person.[11]

If there is a conventional conception of violence it is made up of some mix of the above elements. There is much material already for dispute in what has been said. Yet the most significant areas for dispute have not yet been mentioned. For what is really at issue is how to interpret words like 'inflict', 'destroy' and 'damage' which feature in the account of violence. All these terms are of course descriptions of human *actions*, so that part of what is at issue is a rather theoretical issue concerning the nature of *action* (though the outcome of the issue has some rather practical implications). The following issues have a bearing on our discussion: (1) How far is the notion of *intention* central to the identity of what one *does*? (2) How far is *conscious understanding* of what results from one's acting essential to the identity of what one *does*? (3) How far should one treat the effects of one's omissions as forming part of what one *does* in the world?

A narrow, a wide and a very wide conception of violence will each result, depending on how one answers these questions. If the intention to inflict death is essential to an act's *being* 'an act of inflicting death', then the conception is narrow, and other acts or omissions which, with or without one's knowledge, cause death are not acts of violence at all. If intention and conscious understanding are not essential

125

to 'inflicting death', but one's action or policy is partly
indentified by the actual effects it has in the world, then
a wider conception of violence emerges, as we shall see.
And if inactivity which results in death which would have
been prevented through one's activity is counted as part of
what one does and hence as a form of 'inflicting death',
then such inactivity is a form of negative or quiet violence.
The same set of results would go through for damaging,
degrading and diminishing too.

Institutional Violence

Much violence, albeit unintentioned or unconscious, is done
by people in their personal relationships with one another.
But the most interesting issues arise when one extends the idea
of *inflicting* suffering or harm to the sphere of institutional
relationships, to the effects of laws, established rights,
economic practices or government policies.[12] Thus it may be
said that a repressive regime is violent because it *forces*
poor people to remain poor and hence to die early, to be
damaged and degraded: the regime is violent because it
causes these things to happen, not just when or if it uses
the military to kill or torture people. A system of land
ownership which gives landlords the power to perpetuate the
abject poverty of tenants, is a form of violence, even if
the tenants do not fight back and so there is no 'conspicuous'
violence. A form of rampant capitalism which really
exploits the poor and hence *forces* them to continue in abject
poverty is a form of violence, even if there is no explicit
fighting against it. And if such violence exists within
countries, so too does it exist in international relations
as well. If for instance Western economic practices force
developing countries to accept low prices for their
commodities, then we are indirectly preventing a certain
amount of development and hence condemning many poor people
to early death or degrading lives.

Marxists will no doubt make much of this approach - indeed
it originates out of Marxist thought - and argue that
capitilist economies and non-Marxist forms of government
embody structural violence through and through. But we need
not take such an extreme line in order to find something of
value in the general idea of institutional violence. For
one thing, someone committed to the idea of democracy and
forms of capitalism which are restrained within the enactment

126

of basic rights, free trade unions, proper safety regulations, minimum wage legislation and other features of the welfare state, can find much in the less savoury aspects of capitalism which would merit the label of structural violence. He can clearly so label the practices of anti-democratic regimes, whether of the right or of the left. Thus the practices of communist governments themselves may be criticised, for instance in their institutional violence against the liberties of the individual.

If then one accepts that an action or policy of action is not defined by its avowed aim alone, but is partly defined by its overall consequences, whether these are wanted and foreseen or not, one can see how the idea of causing death, suffering or damage, which is central to the concept of violence, takes on these wider aspects. That however is not the whole story. We do not automatically, if we adopt this extension, call *all* 'causing of suffering or damage' acts of violence. What we do call violence and what we do not call violence depends upon our moral values and judgments about the policies and practices in question. If as seems reasonable to suppose there is a basic core of descriptive meaning to an act of violence, namely that it is the *intentional inflicting of suffering,* then one must add that the way one is prepared to extend the concept to other areas depends on where one thinks *on others grounds* there is a serious evil or injustice involved. That is why a Marxist and a Liberal might agree to extend the idea of violence to non-intentional or systemic cases, but differ about the cases which merit the label.

One important point about the recognition of structural violence centres round one's responses to what is sometimes called 'liberation struggles' against oppressive regimes. The connection with our responses to world poverty is obvious. For one of the aims of many revolutionary struggles has been or is the aim of making greater efforts to tackle absolute poverty, once the oppressive government or colonial power has been removed. For oppressive governments may condone, encourage or even enforce blatant capitalism or racial discrimination, so that the poor are trapped in extreme poverty. (And colonial governments had a tendency to give less weight to the interests and rights of the indigenous people compared with the settlers themselves.)

It is clear that the recognition that an oppressive government is itself practicing *systemic violence* gives strength to the revolutionary cause; for they can argue that it is not they alone who are using violence, but rather the oppressive government who are already using it on a very wide scale. Does this factor give justification to the revolutionary group to pursue its aims through armed struggle? On the one hand, it does not *automatically* give justification. (Let us assume, so as not to deflect from the present issue, that what is *aimed* at is acceptable to us, and not say the instituting of a communist state. The issue here concerns the means.) Justification would not for instance be acknowledged by a pacifist: he might indeed recognise the structural violence of the government but deny that meeting structural violence with armed violence was right. Others can join the pacifist and argue that the case for non-violent resistance is much stronger than is often supposed, as John Ferguson has argued.[13] Furthermore calling oppression 'systemic violence' does not simply equate it with the active violence of killing and maiming or really make it any morally worse than calling it very unjust or wrong - though no doubt there is a temptation in using the terminology to think so.

On the other hand it is vitally important that one does not rush to condemnation of what a revolutionary group may be doing. Anyone who does not have *general* reservations about fighting for just causes, must consider carefully the merits of each case, and he may find that, in consistency, he must not condemn some struggles but even endorse them. Even if, because of general reservations about fighting, one cannot actively endorse such a struggle, one must at least refrain from quick and easy criticism, from the gut reaction of antipathy to conspicuous violence. Talk of systemic violence should serve its purpose: the evil resisted may be *very* bad. What one must certainly not do is to accept or condone what the oppressive government is doing, or if one's own government is, for instance, selling arms to or otherwise helping to prop up the regime, to accept this without question.

We must ask ourselves seriously the question: If we are serious about the alleviation of world poverty, must we not take any effective means that is available? Does this not mean, in this case, opposing the regime whose policies or very existence is one of the chief impediments to such

progress? There can be no doubt about the moral grounds for
putting pressure on such a regime to change. Western
governments, and for that matter individuals, could do a lot
more to exert international pressure upon such regimes, by
castigating their lack of concern for the poor, their poor
record on human rights, and the essential justice of the
cause of liberation struggle (if not of their chosen means).
The effectiveness of international pressure if applied with
earnest could be quite considerable. It is a sober thought
to ponder that if we are in earnest about world poverty, we
should be in earnest to oppose regimes which are oppressive.
And if we are dismayed by the tendency of groups to resort
to violence to fight the oppression of the poor, we will
do more to reduce that tendency if we plead their cause to
the world rather than deplore their violence to our friends.

Omissions

In addition to the extension of violence to the non-
intentional or systemic causing of suffering, there exists
another possible extension of the concept, and that is in
the area of omissions and negative responsibility. This
line, which is favoured by Harris, is that one form of
'inflicting suffering' is precisely to fail to prevent
suffering which one could have prevented. One's inactivity
caused - or contributed to causing - an evil, because one
could have altered the causal conditions by active intervention. Since a sustained policy of omitting to prevent
evils which one could prevent is the product of certain
mental attitudes such as indifference, selfishness and a
commitment to affluence, one can say that these attitudes
are the root cause of one's failing to prevent evils and
hence, by this argument, of one's indirectly causing them.
So selfishness and indifference are the ultimate expressions
of violence.

Such a conclusion is paradoxical. Apart from difficulties
which we need not go into concerning the nature of causality,
violence does seem clearly wedded to the idea of one's
actions *making* something bad happen, to the idea of
coercing or forcing, whether intentional or unintentional,
personal or institutional. Whatever else is said, I do not
make a child in Africa die because I failed to send a £10
cheque that would have saved him. But I do *let* him die -
and if the argument of this book is right, we ought not to

let an awful lot of things happen that do happen. But
'letting happen' is not the same as 'making happen', nor
conversely is preventing an evil the same as avoiding
causing it.

Whether or not it is helpful to extend the idea of violence
to our sins of omission, the discussion does remind us of
several important points. First, our systematic failure to
respond to the needs of others and the indifference or
selfishness which it embodies, do indicate a degree of moral
failing in us. Second, what lies behind the more active
forms of violence such as exploitation and repression are
these general attitudes of selfishness and indifference,
along with more specific feelings of fear, hate and prejudice
These underlying mental causes of active violence take on,
as it were, the hues of violence. So too do our attitudes
of tolerance or indifference when we accept, condone or do
nothing to oppose the practices of others which we know to
be actively violent in the extended sense, whether they be
individuals, institutions or governments. Third, the
discussion reminds us that violence exists on a wide continuum
of cases in many shapes and forms, that there is no clear
cut-off point, and that we live in a violent world, violence
of which is not simply 'out there' but all around us - and
even within us.

Peace and Development

Discussion of violence naturally lead back to the concept of
peace, which can in certain respects be regarded as its
converse. Though the discussion of violence stands as an
independent discussion in its own right, part of what has
emerged from it relates to the theme of the first part of
the chapter, and supports the claim that peace and development are inextrically bound up together. As the Brandt
Report significantly observed, "If reduced to a simple
denominator, this Report deals with peace".[14]

It is important to recognise that Peace is not merely the
absense at any given time of overt conflict or conspicuous
violence. Peace does not really exist for the superpowers
when they are locked in an escalating arms race - not for
nothing is it called the cold war - and peace does not exist
in developing countries if governments feel the need to build
up their armed forces for reasons of internal or external
security. (It is a small irony that Western countries such

as the USA, France and the UK, which supply arms to developing countries, are contributing to the militarisation of those countries and hence the creation of precisely those conditions in which democracy and respect for human rights have difficulty in flourishing.)

The absence of peace in this fuller sense is then a serious impediment to development. For the richer nations' preoccupations with national security and with vast expenditure on armaments mean that contributions to Third World Development are perceived as mere footnotes to foreign policy. And the governments of many developing countries spend high proportions of their limited financial resources on armaments, when health and education programmes are starved of adequate funds.

Conversely it should be added that the absense of development and basic social justice is a serious impediment to peace. So long as the basic aspirations of people are frustrated, so long as the legitimate expectations of countries to a reasonable share in the world's wealth are frustrated, many of the conditions of national and international strife will remain. If you want peace, prepare for development.

But the connection between peace and development is not just a contingent one. For peace, properly understood, must include a commitment to development. A peaceful society is not merely one in which no overt violence occurs: it is one in which human beings flourish in harmony with one another and there is a kind of 'wholeness' - as the Hebrew concept of *shalom* suggests. As John MacQuarrie observed in *The Concept of Peace,* peace is 'love transposed into social and global terms'.[15] A peaceful society cannot really exist unless development has occurred to the extent that the basic rights of all are realised. It cannot be one that contains essentially exploitative economic relations or is controlled by repressive government. It is inconsistent with any form of systemic violence. So too, on a larger scale, would a 'peaceful world' be one in which nations not only lived in harmony with, or at least in respect for, one another, but also cared for the whole global community, and one in which the richer nations were seriously committed to tackling the problems of poverty in the Third World.

Idealistic as this image of peace certainly is, it serves to remind us of the deep connection between peace, justice and development. We must never settle for peace at the expense of justice and development. For at the deepest level we cannot.[16]

PART THREE: WORLD POVERTY AND THE INDIVIDUAL

Chapter 10

ACTIONS AND ATTITUDES

Collective Responsibility

The emphasis in Part II has clearly been placed on global problems and responses to them, and upon what 'we' in the West ought to be doing. The 'we' here covers a number of things. First it includes all of us as a collection of individuals whose actions, attitudes and habits of thought have a wide range of consequences in the world. But just as significantly it includes Western Governments and their departments and related institutions, together with other institutions such as Multinational Companies and Banks. Arguments have been advanced for a variety of changes - for instance, for more Aid, for better Aid, for acceptance of the New International Economic Order, for supporting the U.N. and its Agencies, for curbing the Multinationals, as well as for pursuing disarmament and conservation policies, which also have an important bearing on development issues. All these changes are primarily changes in the policies of Governments and other institutions. We, as a collection of individuals, come into it insofar as we can, in a variety of ways, influence what Governments do.

Such an emphasis upon what *we* in the West ought to do, rather than upon what *each individual* ought to do, is important for two related reasons. First, it is important to realise that we are talking of a vast collective responsibility in relation to a vast problem. The problem cannot be tackled adequately by individuals acting merely in an individual capacity, important as such initiatives are, but requires action on a scale and of a type which necessarily involves action by Governments and institutions backed by public opinion and support. Emphasis upon collective responsibility rather than upon individual duty points to the important fact: there is a problem to be tackled. The central point is that poverty ought to be alleviated, not that you, I or any other individual should do this that or the other. We are concerned with the problem of other people's poverty and how to solve it, not the purity of one's own conscience and how to salve it.

133

Second, we need to know the answer to the 'we' question before answering the 'I' question. Indeed the question "What ought I as an individual to do?" to which we now turn, is an important one. For without the concrete answers given by individuals, a general moral approach, however perceptive will lead to little effective action. But this question can only be answered satisfactorily once one has a clear grasp of what our overall responsibility amounts to, and of how far and in what ways we, either as a collection of individuals or as a Government, fail to fulfil that responsibility This point can be illustrated if we consider the issue of Aid and private giving. Granted that we do have a serious obligation to help alleviate poverty overseas, it is tempting to suppose that one could neatly specify what each person's duty was by formulating a rule for everyone to follow, such as for instance "Everyone ought to give 1% of their income", in the belief that having done that people have discharged their duty to the poor.

But this approach is totally inadequate. First, the problem is not solved by simply giving to charities, but involves government policies, trading and financial arrangements and so on. So any individual who is at all committed will see many things which he ought to do *over and above* any straight-forward giving which he may do. But second, suppose that one could - which one cannot in fact - arrive at a precise percentage of GNP which a rich country ought to give through a combination of private giving and public Aid, such that through so doing it discharged its duty to the poor *fully*. Suppose further that one could arrive at, within the overall percentage ascertained, the proportion that ought to come from private giving and one thus formulated a precise rule like the one above.

Would not the figure or rule decided upon be somewhat academic to anyone at all committed to the cause? For most private individuals would not be giving that amount anyway, or anything like it. So given that the general practice does not result in our 'discharging' our collective duty, a concerned person might decide that he or she ought to give rather more in order as it were to reduce the deficit - but how much more would be a matter for personal decision not a precise rule, since there is no magic percentage figure for compensating for others' negligence. Alternatively, he might do nothing of the kind, but decide that his task is to combat the apathy of those around him who do not acknowledge any duty.

Little is to be gained by trying to calculate a precise percentage - either for individuals or for governments - in order to determine a universal duty. (As a stepping stone the goal of '1% GNP' may nevertheless act as a useful focal point for change.) What is rather more important is that people accept the *general framework* in which certain objectives are perceived as important. Given that perception, the adequacies of people's actions, whether in giving or other kinds of activity, should be assured, though no precise percentages will be relevant. And *if* everyone had the right kinds of moral perception, the 'we' in the West would be doing what we ought and, though no quantification of Aid or Effort would be needed or possible, our collective responsibility would be, and would be perceived to be, adequately discharged. At any rate the whole global situation would be transformed.

What Can One Do?

Let us now turn more directly to the individual. The basic moral argument for commitment has been given earlier and will not be repeated here. The purpose of the present chapter is rather different. It is to explore the *character* of one's moral responses, or the *sort* of moral consciousness which is needed. What, in the last analysis, really counts are certain basic attitudes from which actions flow, rather than detailed specifications of types of action which are our duties.

We can approach this issue conveniently by considering another related question: What *can* individuals do with the goal of reducing world poverty? Answering this question is important for it helps to make clear the possible range of actions open to individuals. To be sure, the fact that one *can* do something does not automatically show that one ought to do it. But one needs to know what one can do, if one is to decide properly what one ought to do. Since it is a generally accepted fact that one cannot say that a man ought to do something he is not in a position to do ('ought' implies 'can', as the philosophical tag goes), it is important to make explicit what can be done. For one of the chief obstacles to people accepting that they ought to do things is the feeling, vague enough and not based on

135

examining the possibilities, that they cannot do these things or at least do them effectively.

The question "What can be done?" is often asked in a despairing tone of voice, as if the person asking it would be only too willing to help combat world poverty, if only there were some way he could. This attitude is really an excuse. It could hardly survive a frank examination of the issue. But it is bolstered up by two commonly held ideas. First, no matter what an individual does, it makes no difference to the overall situation - so why bother? But this rather misses the point of the exercise. No doubt one's 'drop in the ocean' will not abolish hunger nor make a statistically significant difference in the overall problem But if it has contributed to *some* poor people somewhere, though one knows not who they are, living better and more hopeful lives, one has helped.

Second, it is often said that mistakes have been made in Aid giving and by charitable organisations, so that one can never be sure that what one does is actually effective in helping relieve poverty - so there is nothing one can do which is effective. Now undoubtedly there have been and are inadequacies in Aid giving and charity, well recognised by Governments and voluntary organisations. But to use this fact as an excuse for inaction is merely to reveal that one does not think the goal in question is a very serious or important one. For no one takes the possibility of mistakes or failure as a reason for not doing anything if they really value what they are trying to achieve. Taking risks (in the broadest sense) is part of commitment. Consider how a parent would move heaven and earth to find a cure for his child who had a probably incurable disease. Now the value a parent places on his child's good may be exceptional, but it illustrates how generally the degree of effort is as much determined by the value of a goal as by the effectiveness of the available means.

What follows is a schematic semi-formalised representation of the possibilities of action. (Illustrative examples relat to the goal of reducing world poverty: but the schema would of course fit any commitment to a social goal, such as working for Peace, working for a change in attitude towards the environment, working for animal rights or whatever: the details would be different but not the overall schema.)

1. Attitude

Developing and sustaining knowledge and attitudes appropriate to effective actions under 2. This includes:
   (a) knowledge of the general moral arguments, facts about world poverty and about the range of possible actions.
   (b) general moral/spiritual values, appropriate to serious commitment.
   (c) proper understanding of one's own circumstances, strengths and weaknesses, for making one's own moral choices of types of commitment.

2. Action

A. 1. Giving money to assist development
   2. Educating/persuading others who are ignorant or apathetic (either through informal conversation or formal teaching).

3. Political pressure on Governments, multinationals:
   (a) rational persuasion: 'speaking truth to power': letters to M.P.s, petitions.
   (b) non-rational non-violent tactics: e.g. trade boycotts, exposé of corrupt Government practices.
   (c) use of force to achieve ends, e.g. to end oppression of the poor.

4. Other initiatives, e.g. adopting a third world family, starting an alternative trading scheme.

5. Expressing, in one's everyday life, the general life-style or values which are appropriate to people being committed to actions under A. 1-4.

B. 6. Speak in favour of/support ⎫ Organisations which have
   7. Give money to   ⎪ as their objectives one
   8. Join   ⎪ or more of A.1-5 above;
   9. Work actively in   ⎬ e.g. Oxfam (1), World
   10. Work as an employee for   ⎪ Development Movement
   11. Encourage others to do   ⎪ (2,3), Traidcraft (4),
       6-10 vis à vis   ⎭ Churches (5).[1]

What Ought to be Done? Such a schema is not intended to be exhaustive, but simply to indicate the range of types of involvement that are possible. There would of course be wide disagreement about the relative importance of the different kinds of action indicated. Indeed some might be

137

ruled out as not morally acceptable. Supporting armed revolution in a developing country might very well be supporting the most effective way of achieving the relief of poverty (by removing an oppressive regime), but still be ruled out on the grounds that such tactics are morally unacceptable.

Some people might rule out some of the things indicated on the grounds that they are ineffective: a trade boycott on a firm with a bad Third World record may be thought to do no good at all. Others might query the emphasis on life-styles and so on. Again there will be some who believe strongly in charity and see little point in putting pressure on Governments; others on the other hand may believe strongly in such things as the New International Economic Order, and believe that public education and political change are all-important, and charity a side-issue.

Any individual must ask himself two questions here: (i) what is the most effective combination of activities for him to advocate or recommend? (ii) what is the appropriate combination of activities for *him*? These are not the same. It is one thing to have a view about what ought to be done, quite another to believe that one should concentrate on certain things oneself. Unless one keeps these two issues separate there is the danger that one will think that every-one ought to be doing the sorts of things it is suitable for oneself to be doing. At any rate it seems important that one has a view about the range of things to be done, and that that range should be wide and that there be a balance between different kinds of activity. Thus in the present circumstance it is important that some (or most) be more generous, some concentrate on educating the ignorant, some apply pressure on Government and so on. It is not appropriate that everyone should do all these things. Indeed it would be highly inappropriate.

Furthermore in assessing the range and extent of activities which ought to be engaged in, one must take into account certain external considerations, considerations concerning other moral objectives, concerning the basic moral rules and rights which must be followed and respected in whatever one does. It is important that in pursuing a moral objective, one takes care not to take moral short cuts, claiming that the end justifies the means. But more important, in one's enthusiasm for one's chosen concern, one must not forget the importance of other moral objectives which others may choose to pursue. This does not imply that they are important because others have chosen them. Rather in one's *own moral scheme of things* (which we all have, however hazy and unexpressed) there are practices which one regards as central, and objectives which one regards as important for people to pursue, even though one does not choose most of them oneself as one's main concern - indeed one could not.

Thus one may regard many objectives as important to pursue - human rights, animal rights, peace, self-sufficiency, tolerance, penal reform and so on. One may concentrate one's own energies on one or two of these, but it still remains the case that in one's total picture these other things are important as well. One would not for instance, try to deflect someone committed to Amnesty International or the Peace Movement (if these things are important to one's total scheme of things) from these into a World Poverty Movement.

So one's commitment to effective action to combat world poverty should not occur in moral isolation, and could not do so if one has thought the thing out. One must see the thing in perspective and in the context of moral concerns deriving from other parts of one's system of moral thought. Nevertheless, having said that, and having pointed out how the range of effective action one recommends depends upon how one sees the different types of action fitting together and in what order of importance, we should recognize that concern for world poverty should occupy an important position on the total picture. Almost everyone who investigated the issues involved and accepted the general position given in the previous chapters, would acknowledge that, though no precise point can be given for determining what we ought to do, that point is considerably beyond what is generally done now. One reason why the schema puts attitudes before actions, is because, if a person has the right attitudes and knowledge, the right actions will naturally flow from them. Where there's a will, there's a way. Or to adapt another saying: Take care of the attitudes, and the actions will take care of themselves.

Rules, Principles and Personal Choice

What then ought an individual to do? The answer may seem

disappointingly brief: for as a universal or general rule of conduct, very little can be specified except for the general twin injunction 'be knowledgeable' (about the moral and factual issues involved) and 'be concerned'. However these are not really rules in any precise sense anyway, and the main point to note at this stage is a negative point (with immense positive implications): The most important features of a person's commitment do not depend on any general rules or principles but depend upon factors concerning the particular situation and nature of an individual and the choices he makes in the light of them. If one's interest is in some overall moral goal, then one must accept that there will be different responses from different people, according to their position, knowledge, abilities, temperament, their social circumstances, financial resources and so on.

To some extent it is a matter of an individual choosing which concern or which practical measures he will take. Working to alleviate world poverty is certainly not something beyond the requirement of morality nor is it simply benevolence. Nevertheless there is considerable latitude here. One reason why J. S. Mill thought of benevolence as a duty of what he called 'imperfect obligation' was that he thought there was some latitude or degree of choice over the occasions and objects of one's benevolence.[2] This insight can be extended. For there can be a latitude also in the *kinds* of concern one expresses or adopts.

It seems therefore important to recognise the wide scope for moral choice. One cannot lay down a *universal rule:* Everyone ought to do just such and such. If I met someone who devotes himself fully to, say, "Help the Aged", I would not claim that he *ought* to give that up for concern for World Poverty. Again some one in financial difficulties trying to bring up a mentally handicapped child has his or her hands full. To say they ought to do a lot for world poverty would be an impertinence. At a more mundane level, one cannot lay down any exact level of giving, like 'give to poverty overseas 1% of your income'. Such a rule deflects from the real issue, that much needs to be done other than straightforward giving. Furthermore anyone concerned with world poverty would recognise that, given that most people would not actually give that amount, he would need to make a choice - to give more or to educate others or whatever.

However it is worth pausing for a moment to consider the suggestion that people give 1% of their income. For there are good reasons for *adopting* 1% as a personal goal for giving, or as a level of commitment by a particular group, because it is a symbolic gesture towards the Government and a reminder that Western Nations committed themselves in principle in 1971 to total transfers (in Aid, loans and investment) of 1% GNP, of which at least .7% of GNP should be government Aid. By contrast the present level of Aid is about .35%.[3] And 1% may be *chosen* by an individual or a group as the level for a person's commitments and thus '1%' becomes one's *duty* in terms of the ongoing commitment. It may be chosen for the reason mentioned (drawing the Government's attention to *its* actual undertakings), or for other reasons, such as its simplicity or the likelihood of its gaining acceptance. (Another interesting suggestion which I once heard was that one should give 10% of any item which one bought and recognized to be a *luxury*.)[4]

No one however should imagine that '1% GNP' (or .7% Aid) does actually represent the objectively complete extent of Western obligation, somehow pulled out of a moral magic box, or that the moral reasons for choosing a 1% personal commitment involve some universal *rule* about what everyone ought to give, such that if anyone (or everyone) follows the rule, he does his duty by the poor of the world completely. There is no such rule. Indeed part of the underlying approach in this book towards moral consciousness is the rejection of the view which says that our moral commitments can be fully understood in terms of the applications of universal rules. *Much* of morality, roughly the part concerned with conserving the 'social fabric', is concerned with rules of universal application, but much of it is not. There would be neither ongoing cultural vitality nor progress towards a better society, if many people some of their time, and some people much of the time, did not feel personally committed to patterns of activity well beyond the requirements of any universal rules. A Secretary of a Music Society interested in the musical culture of his community no less than an intrepid campaigner for penal reform, puts in many hours of work and effort, because he is interested in pursuing some goal, not in following any rule.

It is a peculiarly one-sided view of morality to think of it only in terms of universal rules and the idea that if anyone

141

ought to do something, then everyone ought to do so - a view of morality which has been encouraged in recent moral philosophy with its fascination for 'universalisability'.[5] However we should think of moral demands (or requirements) and use 'ought' language to express them in other contexts as well, both when we are expressing very general principles of behaviour (which are often called rules, though misleadingly), and when we are expressing personal choices and commitments directed to furthering a moral end which 'ought to be realised' (though by whom and in what ways is left unresolved).

Promoting Justice

Take for example the proposition "one ought to promote justice". This looks like such propositions as "one ought to pay one's debts" and "one ought to tell the truth" but in fact there is a big difference. For whereas the latter specify rules of conduct of a precise nature, the former does not. It is rather a general principle of conduct, which is to be aspired to rather than followed. For it is clear that one could not *completely* follow such a principle, and that how one acts on it depends greatly upon personal choice.

There is of course a sense in which a man might be said to promote or pursue justice *completely* in his life. That is, in his own life he observes the 'rules' of justice and does not act unjustly. He pays his debts, honours his promises, respects other people's rights to privacy and non-interference, is fair in his transactions and in such distributions of good or burdens as it is his duty to determine, and is impartial in his judgments and assessments. Now all this is an important part of justice, but it is only part of the story, both about what justice is all about and what an individual's promoting justice is all about. For on the one hand, there is the justice or injustice of social institutions, or Governments, of laws and of the general practices of people as a whole. And on the other, there is the concern of an individual to promote justice in these things; that is, to support Government, institutions, laws and general practices if or to the extent that they are just, and to work for change in Government, institutions, laws or general practices, if or to the extent that they are unjust.

That is, a moral commitment to promoting justice is only

partly fulfilled by keeping one's own nose clean, so to speak, but it is also significantly concerned with the broader goal of the 'flourishing of justice' in one's society, or in the world. A concern for justice in this sense is not something that can be codified in precise rules. For the variety of things that may be said to be done 'for the sake of justice' may be infinitely wide, and the number of things that could be done for justice's sake is indefinitely large. And what was said about 'as much as one can' theories applies here. It would make nonsense of the moral life if one supposed that it was one's duty to *do all one could* for justice's sake. What the idea of promoting justice provides is an ideal which those concerned with it try to live up to, and towards which they feel a serious obligation to strive.

Discussion of this principle of promoting justice serves two purposes. First, it illustrates the theme that morality should not be thought of exclusively in terms of rules. We do not discharge our moral obligations simply by following the rules which are necessary for social existence. Anyone who is at all concerned with moral goals, like the alleviation of world poverty, or disarmament or the end to the violation of human rights, will recognise a whole new dimension to moral commitment - namely the obligation to play one's part in promoting such a goal. If one fails to observe a rule of justice, e.g. one breaks a promise, one acts unjustly. But if one fails to promote the goal of justice (beyond observing the rules of justice in one's behaviour), one does not act unjustly, though one may fail to take an opportunity for acting 'for the sake of justice'. And if one felt that one ought to have taken it, then one might feel morally inadequate or guilty for not having taken it. But unlike following the rules of justice, which is not a matter for an individual's choice and can be required by others, acting for the sake of justice is more a matter for personal conscience and decision. Beyond pressing the general principle of promoting justice as applicable to everyone, one must leave it to the individual to determine what he does and how much.

Second, it is clear that much of the work done by those concerned with world poverty can be seen in terms of promoting justice, or rather fighting injustice of various sorts. For one can see in the attitudes and practices of people, institutions and Governments much that can be called unjust, or at least inadequate by the standards of justice. If it is a matter of social justice that we ought at all levels to promote the realisation of basic human rights (the right to a decent living and all that that entails), then the general inadequacy of our responses, from the man in the street's indifference to the paltry Aid record of Government, is riddled with injustice (however odd that may sound on first hearing). Furthermore if Governments have been exploitative in their trade policies, or British companies have paid unreasonably low wages to workers in Third World countries, then here are practices which, by the criteria of justice in transactions, are unjust, as are the attitudes and demands for affluence from people which implicitly support or explicitly justify such practices.

One reaction to the perception that there is injustice all around one is to think that one should dissociate oneself from unjust practices. For instance if a firm is thought to be exploitative, one should avoid buying their goods, or sell one's shares if one has any. Or if one thinks that the ruthless pursuit of affluence is the root of evil, one should dissociate oneself from people of that attitude or perhaps escape from the affluent society by joining a simple living commune. Now the impulse to wash one's hands of evil or to clear one's conscience is a natural one but it has limited value.

What is important is not that one ceases to be party to or a beneficiary of injustice, but that one tries to reduce that injustice. Now it may be that some act of dissociation like refusing to buy a particular company's goods *does* reduce injustice and if so, then all well and good. But it is clear that promoting justice by combatting injustice involves a lot more than this, and, can sometimes actually be, if effectively done, inconsistent with dissociation. You salve your conscience be selling your shares, but if they are bought by some who do not care, nothing improves: you might have done better to have kept them and attended an AGM and made your stand. Your turn your back on affluence by retreating into a commune, but thereby you reduce your power to influence the system at all. In any case we are all in it together, and only a very superficial understanding of what it is to be involved with or a beneficiary of evil, injustice or more

144

generally the inadequacies of men, could give one the hope
of a completely clear conscience based on complete
dissociation.

There is quite generally a tension, a pull in different
directions, between the desire to be dissociated from evil
and the desire to tackle and reduce it. One is a desire
for disengagement, the other a desire for engagement. And
though some specific acts of dissociation may be right
because of their contribution towards tackling an evil, the
general direction to be taken by people of moral maturity
and understanding must surely be towards engagement,
towards accepting that we are willy nilly part of an
imperfect world, and towards doing our part to make it less
imperfect.

The Concept of Caring

The preceding discussion of promoting justice serves two
purposes then. It reinforces the point that an important
part of moral commitment lies beyond the observance of
rules: it consists of the pursuit of moral goals which are
felt to be important. The desire to pursue moral goals
derives from certain general attitudes of concern or caring,
and the particular form which the commitment takes depends
largely on the choices of the individual in the light of
his circumstances and abilities. Second, the discussion of
justice reminds us of a point made in Chapter 4, namely that
concern or caring can have a moral dimension and indeed must
have one if it is of the most mature kind. This point is
of some importance and can be illustrated if we take a
longer look at the concept of caring.[6]

There are many words which are used to indicate our positive
responses to other people and their fortunes - caring,
concern, love, agape, loving kindness, kindness, charity,
sympathy, benevolence, humanity and so on. Now there are
undoubtedly many differences of nuance in the way we understand these words. Nevertheless there is a central 'core'
to all of them, namely the idea that a person who has love,
concern or whatever, responds *openly* to others and acts in
ways which are, or at least seem to be, for the *good* of
others. The antithesis to this kind of open-ness is a
reaction to others in which their good is seen as having no
interest for the agent. This may be because he is thinking

in entirely *egoist* terms, i.e. in terms of how *his* interests may be furthered, or because he is blinded to the good of others by particular emotions such as hatred, anger, jealousy or greed. It is probably true that whatever our 'philosophy of life', all people are at least sometimes susceptible to open-ness and caring for others and are at least sometimes susceptible to closed-ness and complete indifference to others. Nevertheless it is important to note that on the whole people differ as to whether their predominant *attitude* towards others is one of openness or is one of closedness.

There are at least three aspects to the basic attitude of caring or concern.

(i) First, at the level which in biological terms is most basic, is what may be called caring for a subjectively valued object. A person may just have an affection or love for another person, for instance a mother for her child. A person is just drawn to another person, wants his good to be realised, values and takes pleasure in its realisation and so on: the reason for this is not based on any belief that his good ought to be promoted or belief that it is his moral duty to promote it. A person just finds in his 'nature' whether genetically implanted or formed through earlier development, a desire directed outwards onto some other being

(ii) Second, a person may care for another person out of a recognition of the objective value of the wellbeing of that person. With the development of a certain degree of maturity a person comes to recognise that the good of another person is not something which is simply *of value* because it happens to be *of value to him,* i.e. happens to be subjectively valued by him, but it is also something which is 'obejctively good, something which ought to exist, or is better existing than not existing. Furthermore, since it ought to exist, he ought to further its existence, insofar as he is in a position to do so and other things are equal. Thus one's caring for another's good has taken on a simple *moral* dimension, and is related to the basic if somewhat simple principle discussed earlier that one ought to promote human good.

(iii) Third, a person's caring may take on a more sophist-icated 'moral' aspect, insofar as his promoting another man's good is informed by the belief that so doing is his duty, a requirement of justice or of respect for another man's rights, or the application of a moral rule which applies to the circumstances. At this level the focus is not so much on the *good* one is promoting as on the fact that one's promoting the good is required by moral considerations. Furthermore the 'good' which is being promoted may itself be largely understood in moral terms. The aspect of good involved might be for instance the relief of pain, the provision of food and shelter, but it might also be, for instance, removing injustice and exploitation, establishing respect for people's rights, giving people political freedom or autonomy. Promoting another man's good in such respects presupposes that both the promoter and receiver of help understand, and are influenced by, a sophisticated system of moral thought.

These different levels of caring are typically blended together, and indeed the richest manifestations of caring are those in which they are blended together, particularly the subjective and objective aspects. It is of course possible for someone to care for another entirely from subjective attraction or love. The danger of this is that without a concern for the real 'good' of the other person, as opposed to what is valuable to oneself in one's state of attraction, one's caring may do no good and slip into egoistic self-gratification. On the other hand, if one's caring is only actuated by moral reasoning or the detached thought that objective good is being promoted, one's caring may be cold and lacking in the subjectivity of warmth and pleasure which are also important in human relations.

Furthermore direct caring for another's good and indirect caring through acting on moral considerations are both important as well. For the latter without the former would lose sight of the central fact that it is *another human being's good* to which one is responding, and the former without the latter would lack a sufficiently sophisticated understanding both of what good consists in and the reasons for promoting it. An adequate person need not show in his caring all these aspects at all times. But they must all be aspects of his general attitudes of caring and must sometimes be blended together. Another way of indicating the general thrust of this discussion is to say that 'love' and 'justice' are both essential to morality. Love without justice becomes sentimental and unstructured, justice without love becomes cold and inflexible. Or to put the point in another way:

love and justice in their fullest forms each include the other.[7]

The Sense of Responsibility

If we want a summary to this chapter it is simply that basic caring, informed by a concern for justice, will lead to adequate forms of action. Attitudes then are the important thing. But it is not just the basic attitudes of caring and concern for justice which are important. Discussion in other parts of the book has shown that other related attitudes are also relevant - optimism, courage and a willingness to think internationally. The latter is a willingness to think of oneself, politically, as a world citizen, and, morally, as sharing a common humanity with the rest of humankind.

This sense of sharing a common humanity might also be called 'a sense of broad responsibility'. This idea of responsibility lies beyond the more limited idea of moral responsibility, i.e. of what we have a duty to do. It is the idea that because of our power of agency to affect the lives of countless others, we are somehow 'responsible for' the world. It involves the recognition of the essential 'connected-ness' of human beings, and of the seminal idea that 'no man is an island'. But more than that, it is expressive of a certain 'open-ness' to, or caring for, the good of others. Having this attitude does not mean that one thinks one *ought* - in the sense of moral duty - to promote *any* good or reduce *any* evil simply because we can. But we recognise that the good or ill of another person does, in principle, give us reason to act, in the sense that it is intelligible that we should care for the good of others in our actions. This basic *orientation* is fundamental, for it is only within this wider framework that an appropriate system of moral thought can develop. It is the soil in which moral consciousness thrives.

The contrast to this awareness of broad responsibility is a sense of narrow or limited responsibility. The latter is not the idea of moral responsibility. Rather it is again a general approach to life, and is marked by the antitheses to what has been mentioned. In this approach people are regarded as essentially disconnected and isolated, and every man is an island. The essential attitude is one of closed-ness. There is a suspicion of others' intentions,

148

scepticism over the power of agency, and a rejection of the idea that the good of others gives one any reason to act. In short the focus of responsibility is oneself. Such a person may indeed have a kind of moral code in which he recognises duties and specific moral responsibilities, but his sense of responsibility - of what he is in a general way responsible for in the world - brings him back to that isolated unit called himself.

This discussion of broad responsibility illustrates the earlier contention that what at the end of the day matters is a person's general attitudes. It matters that he has a general propensity for caring and that he accepts certain broad principles of conduct, beyond the requirements of specific rules. If these are adequate, then the actions needed to combat world poverty or tackle other social problems will be forthcoming.

Some would no doubt argue that behind the general attitudes which have been described there must lie some spiritual or religious experience or outlook. They may say that in the end little change will take place in our actions and policies without a large spiritual or religious renewal or revival.[8] If this claim is simply or primarily that we need a recognition of values other than those of an intensely materialistic kind, then there is no disagreement with the general thesis of the book. But if this claim is meant to mean that we need the explicit acceptance of Christian theology or that of some other religion, then it must be observed that the discussion has not rested on such foundations. The general attitudes of caring, moral seriousness and broad responsibility are powerfully sustained by religious experience and belief in many - though not all - forms.[9] But they have an independent and self-authenticating value as well, and it is on these terms that they have been presented in this chapter. How far people may be persuaded to adopt and act on these attitudes will be the issue we face in the final chapter.

Chapter 11

HAVE WE THE WILL?

What are the chances of a major transformation of attitude and action in the Western world towards the problems of world poverty? The reader of this book, if he or she has stayed to this point, may very well be sympathetic to the general thesis and may indeed be inclined to do various things for world development. But he or she may still be disturbed by the thought that it is quite unrealistic to suppose that the vast majority of people in industrialised countries will do anything very much about it. Yet in the face of this thought one can remain sufficient of an optimist to believe in the real possibility of changes of attitude and of changes in the patterns of action which flow from them. In this chapter we will give some backing to this optimism by trying to show that the factors which make people resistant to having adequate responses to such problems as world poverty are not cast-iron or immovable factors in the human make-up but are capable of modification and transformation.

How Far are Changes of Attitudes Possible?

We must be wary of one common pitfall into which unwary idealists are liable to fall. It may be called the 'some-all' fallacy. Idealists commonly argue that the world would be a better place if everyone or at least most people did what they recommend or acted upon the values they accept, and support their claim by pointing to the evident fact that *some* people already *do* act in these ways and that it is therefore possible for everyone to do likewise. Unfortunately the last proposition does not follow. One cannot argue from the fact that some people *can* do something to the fact that all (or most) people can do the same thing. Hermits can (because they do) live and choose to live in utmost simplicity and isolation from fellow human beings, but it is doubtful that most human beings could do so. What of course renders them unable to do so is not any technical inability or lack of skill but rather the absence of appropriate motivational resources.[1]

It is not being claimed that when an idealist recommends that people should generally behave in a certain way which is different from the established practice, he must be wrong to suppose that what he recommends could happen. He may be right or he may be wrong. What he cannot do is assume that he is right because he knows that some people, including himself no doubt, do behave in that way. Whether most people 'have it in them' to do so is an open question. This phrase points to what is the key issue: how far and in what directions can people's motivational resources and dispositions be modified? How far, that is, do people have 'in them' the psychological adaptability necessary for significant motivational changes to take place?

In the discussion that follows a number of ways will be suggested in which people's motivational interests could be so modified as to lead to greater responses to world poverty. How far they will be is another matter. That depends partly upon how many people take it upon themselves to educate, motivate and encourage others. But who or what, one may ask, motivates the motivators? Again it may be other committed people acting as catalysts... But it may just be the primary impulse of concern, experience and moral conviction, which must start somewhere but which one hopes will spread by a contagion or snowball effect through the successive agents of change.

Three Obstacles

There are, I would submit, three main reasons why people generally do not respond very much to the challenge of world poverty, or to the challenges presented by many other social evils for that matter.
(i) People are generally very ignorant of the basic facts about world poverty, about the extent of Western involvement and so on. Ignorance or a smattering of knowledge is hardly an adequate basis for genuine or significant responses.
(ii) People generally do not care enough about the wider world around them. This may be because they are not caring people at all, or because the areas in which they show their concern are strictly limited to a few people, such as family and friends.
(iii) People have not generally assimilated the moral arguments for helping to alleviate world poverty.

This third fact may be because they have not really thought about them, or if they have thought about the moral issues, do not accept the moral arguments. Or, perhaps more significantly, they do more or less accept that there are

151

moral arguments, but these moral arguments do not lead to
significant action. The two main reasons for this are that
commitment to such an objective is seen as conflicting with
a person's interests or the quality of his life as he perceives it, and that there is nothing in his life through
which he can identify himself with these values. Both these
reasons point to the more general factor, that though the
person may intellectually accept the moral arguments, there
is nothing (or little) in his *moral experience* or his moral
consciousness which gives him the motivational energy to
act on the values he accepts. One might say that what he
accepts with his head he does not accept in his heart. But
this, though half right, is misleading, since there is no
simple 'reason-emotion' contrast nor is it simply a matter
of emotional engagement, but a matter of a total engagement
of the whole person. That is why the broad phrase 'moral
experience' is used.

Ronald Higgins, in *The Seventh Enemy,* points to the same
three factors when he writes:

> We saw earlier that much political inertia results from
> the blindness of individuals whether as rulers or ruled.
> I attribute this blindness to three prime causes:
> failure in comprehending the facts, failure to make
> appropriate moral judgments, and failure to sustain
> sympathy, the energizing power behind all saving action.[2]

His own discussion of ways of 'countering individual blindness', which is considerably more detailed than what follows
is well worth reading, and supports the contention that it
is *reasonable* to suppose that people's attitudes could be
changed in all the respects just indicated. That is to
say, if people were generally better informed, then on the
whole they would be more inclined to respond positively to
the problems. If people cared more or more widely about
the world around them, they would respond more positively;
people can be encouraged to be more caring. If people can
be persuaded of the moral arguments, or can come to see
that responding to world poverty does not conflict with
their quality of life, or can come to identify themselves
more fully as members of a world community, then much more
would be done about the problems of world poverty. Let us
look at these different points in greater depth.

The Need for More Knowledge

Relatively little needs to be said about the necessity for

152

people to be better informed. It seems clear at any rate that without knowledge of a situation, one cannot respond to it. On the other hand it must be added that knowledge by itself will not lead to action: a person with no natural or moral concern about a social problem might be an expert on that problem and yet do nothing about tackling it. Experts can sometimes be depressingly detached from any practical or evaluative implications of the object of their study. Nevertheless it remains a valid generalisation that knowledge and information are essential to effective action, not only in specifying accurately the appropriate means to take, but also in activating people's general concern and basic moral values into commitments in certain specific directions.

It is worth adding in passing that if one's concern is to promote knowledge or understanding, one must acknowledge the vital role of free and critical discussion. People on the whole do not learn about things by being handed information, let alone understanding, on a plate for consumption, but by critically responding to and being encouraged to critically respond to the ideas which are presented. (This is true not just of informal communication but also of formal education in schools - a fact often forgotten however by education-alists.) Freedom of thought and discussion not only has immense intrinsic value (as one of the elements of human good), it is also vital for the growth of the kind of know-ledge with which we are concerned, and the importance of free discussion as a vehicle of communication must not be overlooked.

It is of course to be granted that if free discussion is encouraged, the outcome of such discussion, in terms of what the participants believe about the facts or values after it, may not always be in line with what the person committed to development believes or wants people to believe. Again one must observe that though there is always the perennial risk that people acquire the wrong 'knowledge' from the creative interplay of ideas, this risk must be taken in the firm belief that free discussion does overall promote genuine knowledge or truth and does it better than indoctrination or thought control. Of course the 'facts' about the Third World, about the West and about the global situation which give rise to our obligations to assist the Third World, *might* not be facts. A quite different 'Truth' might come out. But that possibility will never deter the promulgation of what one takes to be knowledge or the pursuit of a goal based on that knowledge. A committed life is always, in one sense, a hostage to the fortunes of Truth.

Caring and Self-fulfilment.

If we turn to the fact that many people do not care all that much about wider social issues, or rather about the people whose problems and ills collectively make up these issues, we may wonder whether there is much that can be done about this? Are not people either the caring type or not the caring type? There is some truth in this sobering verdict, yet there does seem to be some scope for changes in attitude. In addition to the points made in the last chapter about the concept of caring, two arguments can be mentioned which may help to persuade at least some people that there is something to be said for the attitude of caring. The arguments do not relate specifically to concern for world poverty, but their relevance will be apparent. The two arguments are linked, but there is a difference of style to them, which reflects the differences between the two thinkers from whom they are derived.

In *Man for Himself* Eric Fromm, the Austrian philosopher psychologist argued that a life of love or openness to others was in fact the kind of life in which man realised himself most fully or found self-fulfilment.[3] He opposed the idea that serving others or more generally doing one's duty was a form of self-denial or contrary to one's own interests. He claimed that it was a deep psychological truth that man is so constituted that his real interests or what constitutes his well-being or happiness consists precisely in relating to others in relationships of love and caring. Fromm was well aware that most people are quite blind to this fundamental truth. In many of his writings, particularly his last book *To Have or To Be,* he argued that the values of Western materialistic society with its emphasis upon consumption or 'having' obscured the truly more important value of 'being' or relating openly to other human beings.[4]

Fromm formulates well a theme that has had a perennial appeal to many thinkers throughout the ages. It contains of course a serious attack upon an egoist approach to life. Someone who relates only or largely to his fellow men in terms of what *he* gains by way of pleasure of advancement of his interests is just cut off from one of the major and

indispensable sources of satisfaction and fulfilment.
This is true. But one must note a light air of paradox
which creeps in here. For if a life of caring is a life
in which one best fulfils oneself then it is surely in one's
interests to lead a life of caring! The paradox is
instructive insofar as it shows *where* such a consideration
of one's interest is relevant. It is also harmless,
provided one's recognition of the fact does not mean that
one deliberately engages in caring with the express purpose
of fulfilling oneself. For that would not *be* caring, only,
as it were, going through the motions of caring. Nor would
it be the source of self-fulfilment intended either.

The contrast with egoism is made more explicit by another
philosopher, namely Thomas Nagel in *The Possibility of
Altruism,* a difficult book but containing a wealth of
insights.[5] I do not pretend to give a proper account of
his doctrine, but simply adapt for my own purpose several
of his points. He argues that the essential difference
between an egoist and a person with proper moral awareness
such as an altruist is that, whereas the egoist only
recognises his own good, desires or interests as giving
him reason to act, the altruist sees the good or interests
of others as giving *him* a reason to act, namely to promote
what they have reason to get. Whereas the egoist only
acknowledges subjective reasons and values, the altruist
accepts objective reasons and values. Here Nagel gives one
particular expression to the powerful idea of Immanuel
Kant, that as moral agents we ought, rationally, to treat
other people as ends in themselves, not merely as means.[6]
His argument also gives theoretical support for the principle
of promoting human good, which has occupied a significant
place in the previous discussions.

The significance of Nagel's arguments in the present context
is this. He argues that the consequence of failing to
acknowledge objective reasons and values (e.g. that another
man's good is objectively valuable) is that one falls into
what he calls 'practical solipsism'.[7] That is, one in
effect denies, or fails to make sense of, in the fullest
sense, the *practical reality* of other people. By failing
to see other people as sources of practical demands upon
one, one does not see them as real or rational agents. This
is a difficult idea but it is essentially sound. Of course
one can say that an egoist sees other people around him;

but there is a sense in which he cannot relate to them as he would if he acknowledged that their good was of objective value. He would in a sense be isolated by his own egocentricity.

One might also add, though Nagel does not say this, that a consistent egoist (whom Nagel thinks is hardly a real possibility) would be debarred from participating in any discussions about the common good or moral goals since he denies the existence of the point of view from which these make sense. He would also fail to value himself as having objective value and hence as being an object of respect for others, since he denies the possibility of objective value.

These remarks then all point to the same general verdict: the 'costs' involved in failing to relate fully to others, in the lack of real self-value and so on are high. The alternative to egoism is of course acknowledging and promoting the good of others, where that good is seen as objectively valuable. We can thus see further confirmation for the view that caring for others, which *must include* the objective levels mentioned earlier, is a natural attitude and one that is psychologically speaking more healthy than the attitude of egoism.

The arguments for the importance of caring for others in one's life do not of course point directly towards caring for the poor of the world. There is no doubt that a person could be a very caring person and yet do nothing at all about world poverty. Yet the general conclusion is very useful, since it shows the general propriety of caring, which for many may find its natural expression in the sphere of world poverty, especially in view of the extremity and extent of that poverty. However there is a particular respect in which the last argument has a more specific relevance to the argument of this book. For if to reject the egoist approach is to accept the idea of objective value, then it follows that one accepts that *any* man's good is, *in principle,* something to be promoted, whether that man is next door, in one's own country or in a developing country. There is no half way house position, according to which the good of only *some other* human beings (those of one's own country perhaps) is of objective value or gives one reason to act. So the force of this argument is to render untenable any *selective* altruism or caring as a principle of action. (Of course in

156

practice, one is selective about one's main concerns, and
this is natural and inevitable.)

The recognition that in principle any person's good may give
one reason to act indicates an attitude of practical 'openness' which has links with the sense of broad responsibility,
discussed in the last chapter. For the sense of broad
responsibility, which is distinct from the moral senses
connected with culpability and obligation, is the awareness
that one has it in one's power almost constantly to do so
many things pertaining to the well-being of an indefinite
range of human beings. It is this awareness which expresses
one's openness to and sense of being connected to human kind
at large. It is at one and the same time both a necessary
background feature of adequate moral experience, and an
important part of the consciousness in which men can find
their self-value. By contrast, the man with a sense of
narrow responsibility sees what is in his power as centring
upon himself and little more, and he does not see further
because of the essential closedness of his outlook.

Ideals and Requirements

One of the reasons why less is done for the sake of world
poverty than might be done, is because people either do not
acknowledge the moral arguments, or if they do, they are not
motivated to act upon them. What are the problems involved?
Insofar as people may be either ignorant of the moral
argument or inclined to reject them, nothing can be added at
this stage of the discussion, since the whole book has been
concerned to present the moral arguments in some depth.
There are no doubt simpler ways of making the moral points
which would be more effective with most people, but that is
up to those who are more skilled in popular communication!
However one hidden reason why many of those who do not accept
the moral arguments do not do so, is because they do not
feel they would have the psychological resources or the will
to *act* on them if they did accept them. So if anything below
helps to establish possible motivation, it will be of
relevance to any arguments about the moral issues themselves.

Why then is it that many people may accept that there are
moral arguments for helping combat world poverty, but nevertheless do nothing or very little about it? No doubt one of
the factors involved is the tendency to think of the moral

reasons in terms of *ideals* rather than here-and-now *requirements*. It is very easy to slip into a way of thinking like "Well, of course we ought to be doing an awful lot to help the poor overseas, but in our actual situation there are other priorities - the rates need paying, the grass needs cutting and I really can't do without a hi-fi for much longer". What we 'ought to do' then is a vague abstaction, what we would do if ..., and something we certainly do not feel bad about not doing nor something anyone else thinks badly of us for not doing.

However the argument of this book has been that, even if the obligation to help is not something which has a precise specification concerning when or how it is to be done, it is nevertheless a *serious* one. One of the motives behind the common argument of developmentalists that it is a matter of *justice* not charity that we do more for developing countries is to make the point that such action is a moral requirement not an optional expression of an ideal. For justice is typically something which is required or demanded, and charity is often seen as 'beyond duty' or an expression of an ideal. The motive behind this terminological move is a good one. It does not however settle very much; for one can also distinguish justice as an ideal from justice as a here-and-now requirement, and on some theories, notably Christian ones, charity may be regarded as a strict duty.[8]

What then if one does accept that one ought to help alleviate world poverty, in the sense that it is some kind of obligation, not just an expression of an ideal? Some philosophers, notably R. M. Hare in *Freedom and Reason*, would argue that if I accept that I *ought* (morally) to do something then I must, on pain of inconsistency, act (or try to act) as I think I ought: the sign of sincerity in accepting the moral judgment is that I do act on it.[9] This view known as 'prescriptivism' would, if it were correct, settle the problem of moral motivation very quickly. It does not however seem to be correct. For it is precisely in the sort of area where people acknowledge that they have obligations in relation to large but vague moral goals, that the issue of motivation becomes most problematic.

It is no doubt true of some moral principles, those which are most central to a person's values and his emotional identity, that a decision not to act on them would call into question the agent's sincerity, or at least require special explanation. But it is clear that many of the obligations which a person quite genuinely acknowledges are not like this: they may or may not be acted upon depending on varied circumstances. The fact that our obligation to help alleviate world poverty is, though serious, not generally strictly specified but involves a fair degree of choice and flexibility, illustrates a sad fact. It is all too easy to find reasons for putting off to another occasion the discharging of an obligation.

Self-Interest

Let us now turn to the two reasons mentioned earlier why people may fail to act on moral arguments which they may, at least at an intellectual level, accept. One reason why people may be reluctant to act on moral arguments which they accept but which they do not regard as absolutely central to their values, is that they are inclined to believe that acting on them would seriously conflict with their interests. Now there are two points that need to be made about this.

(i) In Chapter 6 we saw that though there are important arguments to the effect that it is in our Western interests to encourage development and reform the international economic system, it does not follow that it is in the same straightforward way in the interests of an *individual* to make large contributions to development. For such an action, in the absence of a general level of such giving, would not result in proportional economic returns for him. Nevertheless, the fact that what he is doing is *also* a contribution to Britain's (longterm) economic well-being, in which he certainly has an interest, may be an additional source of motivational interest and supplement the interest which he has in the moral arguments.

(ii) Suppose therefore that an individual accepts that he ought to make a significant financial contribution. (Even giving 1% of one's income, though proportionally very small, is significant for it is enough for most people to *feel* the loss of what they might otherwise have spent on other things.) Or, suppose that he thinks he ought to devote some of his spare time to work relevant to development. Do these actions conflict with his interests? They certainly conflict with his interest in having as much money as possible and his interest in doing other things with his time respectively. It is certainly significant that even if one has no immediate desire to spend spare money on something, the interest most people have in keeping money on one side for something later or investing it for *future* financial security is an important one. Nevertheless it is surely arguable that if one asks oneself the question: "What is in my interests, in the sense that *without it* the quality of my life would be damaged or that what is important to me in life would be threatened?", it would be difficult for most people to answer that that 1% contribution was essential to their interests. If that was their honest answer then the chances are that they are not the people whose consciences need stirring. Or alternatively, if they answered that it was, they would probably have a *very* materialistically oriented set of values with a great sense of insecurity thrown in. In which case one would have to question their whole understanding of the quality of life.

At any rate the general point is the same as the one made in the second chapter on the Environment, that if we have a proper understanding of what is essential to human flourishing or the quality of living, we will realise that much of the trappings of affluence is not essential to our well-being, however much our habituation to it makes things seem otherwise. (Note also Fromm's distinction between 'being' and 'having', referred to above.) Furthermore if what has been said about caring for others is at all right, working at something relevant to development may be quite as rewarding as the sorts of activities usually associated with pursuing one's own interests - particularly if one participates in the sense of cooperation and joint effort which working for an organisation often involves.

International Identity

The other reason why people are not very motivated to pursue development goals leads us into a quite new and important area of discussion. It is no doubt true that there are some people who are strongly motivated in this area simply by their concern for the immense suffering involved. But for many people what is needed is something which makes the issues more psychologically alive or vivid for them in their moral experience. This may happen through some accident of personal history, like reading a disturbing book, seeing a film, meeting a family from a poor country. And it is perhaps significant, if sadly so, that many of those most active in development activities turn out to have had some experience in a developing country in their past.

This leads to the more general point that people need to *identify* in some way with what it is they are concerned about. It appears to be a general feature of moral concerns that they are attached to specific and identifiable parts of a person's 'social reality'. It is no accident for instance that people recognise their duties and obligations in relation to organisations, groups, communities, established roles such as father or teacher, accepted rules and institutions, or their church and its body of public theology. A person's relation to such things provides many of the marks or features of his own sense of identity, and his sense of what he ought to do is securely anchored to these features. One of the problems with concerns such as a concern over world poverty is that the appropriate marks in a man's 'social reality' relevant to his identifying himself with the issue, and thus being morally motivated, are often not well established.

This can be illustrated by the contribution made by religion. In a sense the religious person has available the appropriate marks with which to identify. For instance the public and shared idea of the 'brotherhood of man', backed and enriched by a strong theology, is an important inspiration for a religious person. So too is the fact that the Church, to which he *belongs,* is a world wide social entity spanning the gap in psychological terms between where he is and where the poverty to which he is responding exists. This may partly explain why religious people are in the vanguard of those concerned with development.

What is lacking is, one might say, a strong secular counter-part. The counterpart already exists of course. For it is the United Nations and its many important Agencies. But the U.N. is not strong enough nor given enough support. Again what we need is not only the existence of this international system, we need a corresponding *international ethic,* the equivalent of a shared public theology, a set of well established and agreed principles which are known by people in general and shared with other people. So that when an individual is inclined to act, he does so in the knowledge that he acts from an agreed international ethical standpoint and that in so acting he acts in solidarity with mankind and as a world citizen. The concept of a 'world citizen' is at the moment an idealist abstraction which can have little psychological reality for all but the very few whose response to moral ideals is well developed.

It may help to clarify this idea if we draw on an analogy which Bradley made in *Ethical Studies*.[10] He argued that a living morality had two parts to it: on the one hand there are the numerous moral wills of the individual members of a society, which he compared to the soul, and on the other hand, there are the public institutions and rules of the society, which he compared to the body. Just as a living person needs soul and body, so a living morality need both the moral wills of individuals and the 'social reality' of public institutions and rules. It is probable then that the degree of commitment to third world development will never be very extensive, except for the commitment of the morally dedicated, unless the 'public' correlate to the 'private' wills of individuals is properly developed. This public correlate is the institutions of internationalism notably the United Nations and related bodies, and established principles and attitudes of internationalism which inform and justify support for those institutions.

There are many reasons for supporting the United Nations system, not least because in quite practical terms it provides the main hope for maintaining international peace and it provides through its many agencies large opportunities for development programmes.[11] But the point stressed here is the rather different one. Apart from any specific good it directly does, the U.N. is also the external or public *embodiment* of the spirit of internationalism and of the possibility of a truly international ethic. This we desperately need, not least for the reason that the better such an ethic is established, the more ready individuals would be to hang part of their moral identities upon it and act positively for the goals it recommends. So any concern we have for encouraging people in general to act positively for international goals will in practice have partly to concentrate on strengthening knowledge of and support for these international institutions and the principles which underlie them.

This book can be at one level be summed up as a 'plea for internationalism'. Genuine internationalism is the main-spring for serious commitment to development. For the international outlook puts equal value on all human beings, sets no great store on nationalistic values or identities, and shows openness to humanity at large. It is powerfully sustained by the attitudes of caring and moral concern for justice on a global scale. In a world of crisis it is also sustained by the attitudes of hope, trust and courage. These attitudes are important, not just because they contribute to commitment to development, but because our collective global interests require them.

All these attitudes, like caring itself, are not only the appropriate moral responses to the global crisis which we face, they also contribute to the self-fulfilment of the agent whose attitudes they are. The quality of life is enhanced by the attitudes of caring, hope, courage and trust, as it is blunted by the attitudes of indifference, despair, fear and distrust. Our world is indeed a dangerous and tragic world to live in, but let us respond to it with those qualities of mind which make it a better place to live in and at the same time make our own lives more worth living.

Chapter 1

1. See, e.g., *North-South: A Programme for Survival*, the Report of the Independent Commission on International Development Issues under the Chairmanship of Willy Brandt (Pan Books 1980), p. 50. This Report will be referred to as *The Brandt Report*.
2. R. Macnamara, *Address* to the Board of Governors of the World Bank, 30th September, 1980.
3. *New Internationalist*, No. 68, October 1978, p. 8.
4. J. Ferguson, *Disarmament The Unaswerable Case*, (Heinemann 1982) p. 78.
5. G. Foggan, interviewed by J. Burke in *The Survival Game*, 'How can I survive without a job?' (C.E.W.D.E., 25 Wilton Road, London, SW1V 1JS).
6. T. Honderich, *Violence For Equality*, (Penguin Books 1976) p. 19.
7. See, e.g. J. Taylor, *Enough is Enough*, (SCM Press 1975) p. 10, quoting from *The Environment: A Radical Agenda*, BSSRS Paper No. 1, 1972.
8. R. Sider, *Rich Christians in an Age of Hunger*, (Hodder and Stoughton 1977) pp. 37-8.
9. *The Brandt Report*, p. 244 ff. See also quotation from Barbara Ward in Chapter 4.
10. The distinction between the Right/conservative and the Left/radical is not intended to fit neatly political parties. Many people in all political parties would in fact subscribe to the 'reforming' approach defended here.
11. See E. F. Schumacher, *Small is Beautiful* (Blond and Briggs 1973).
12. The 'NIEO' was adopted by the UN General Assembly in 1974 as a Programme of reform to the world economy, so that poorer nations benefitted more from world trade. Little has been done as yet to implement it. See, e.g. *Towards a World Economy that works*, (UN Department of Public Information, New York, 1980).
13. These themes are well brought out in Willy Brandt's Introduction to *The Brandt Report*, pp. 7-29.
14. Barbara Ward, quoted in *World Goodwill* Paper, July 1980.
15. The term 'development' is itself open to differing interpretations. Some of these differences relate to the goal, some to the means. Briefly, my view is that

development as a goal should be seen, in the context of poor countries, as the sustainable improvement of living standards for very poor people, rather than increase in a country's GNP as such. (See e.g. Chapter 6 for further discussion.) *How* such improvements in the living standards of the very poor is to come about, what social and economic changes are needed etc., are questions not pursued here. Clearly though it is not just a matter of transferring money from the rich to the poor.

* * *

Chapter 2

1. J. Bentham, *Introduction to the Principles of Morals and Legislation,* (1789). Reprinted, e.g. in *Utilitarianism,* ed. M. Warnock (Fontana 1962).
2. J. S. Mill, *Utilitarianism,* (1859). Reprinted, e.g. in Fontana edition.
3. See, e.g., J. C. C. Smart, *Utilitarianism For and Against,* (Cambridge U.P. 1973). B. Williams provides useful criticisms in the 'Against' half.
4. Some of the variations concern the role of rules. For a detailed discussion of the differences between 'Act' and 'Rule' Utilitarianism, see e.g., J. Lyons *Forms and Limits of Utilitarianism,* (Oxford, 1965).
5. For a forthright application of the Utilitarian approach to world poverty, see P. Singer 'Famine, Affluence, and Morality' *Philosophy and Public Affairs,* I, No. 3, 1972. Reprinted in *World Hunger and Moral Obligation,* ed. W. Aiken and H. La Follette (Prentice-Hall, 1977). See also Chapter 8 'Rich and Poor' in Singer's book *Practical Ethics,* (Cambridge U.P. 1979).
6. See, e.g., W. Frankena *Ethics,* 2nd Edition (Prentice-Hall 1973) and J. Rawls *A Theory of Justice* (Harvard U.P. 1971), sections 5, 6, 29, 30 for critical discussion.
7. J. Harris *Violence and Responsibility* (Routledge & Kegan Paul 1980), especially Chapters 1, 2 and 9.
8. T. Honderich, *Violence For Equality* (Penguin Books 1976) Chapters 1 and 2.
9. Similar issues are raised when we consider 'The Arms Race Kills' and Violence in Chapter 9.
10. J. B. Priestley, *An Inspector Calls* (Heinemann 1947)

provides a powerful statement in drama form of the idea
of extended responsibility.

* * *

Chapter 3

1. See, e.g., H. Bull, 'Human Rights and World Politics'
   in *Moral Claims and World Affairs*, ed. R. Pettman
   (Croom Helm 1979) for a critical discussion of
   universal rights.
2. See, e.g., L. Levin *Human Rights, Questions and Answers*
   (Unesco Press 1981) for a sympathetic interpretation of
   UN Rights. See also *Human Rights and World Order*,
   ed. A. A. Said (Praeger 1978).
3. This book is an exercise in 'normative ethics', that is
   in presenting arguments for a moral point of view. It
   does not deal with 'meta-ethical' issues, e.g. the
   nature of moral judgment - whether subjective or
   objective - or moral methodology. But briefly for those
   interested, my approach is that moral judgments are not
   subjective in the sense that they depend upon the
   particular feelings or desires of the person who makes
   them. They are objective, not primarily in the sense
   that they point to some supra-human realm of values
   (though there is something in this), but in the sense
   that they are formed by a process of rational and
   critical reflection on the data of experience. Through
   this we attempt to harmonise a wide range of views -
   strongly held particular judgments, general moral
   principles, general views of human nature and of society.
   These are all adjusted and refined so as to achieve a
   state of 'reflected equilibrium'. The two types of
   moral relationship in which we stand to other human
   beings and which are presented in the text are
   arguably part of the full moral theory that emerges.
   For the idea of 'reflective equilibrium' see J. Rawls
   op. cit. section 9. For differing conceptions of
   objectivity see, e.g. J. L. Mackie, *Ethics* (Penguin
   1977) Ch. 1, and T. Nagel 'The Limits of Objectivity',
   Tanner Lectures on Human Values, ed. S. M. McMurrin
   (University of Utah Press and Cambridge U.P., 1980).
4. See, e.g. J. Finnis, *Natural Law and Natural Rights*
   (Oxford 1980) for a modern discussion of Natural Rights.
   See also R. Tuck *Natural Rights Theories* (Cambrdige U.P.

1979).

5. See J. Finnis, *op. cit.* Ch. IV, on of the impoitance
   of the idea of different aspects of human good.
6. E. Fromm, *Man For Himself* (Holt, Rinehart and Winston
   1947). See also Chapter 11.
7. See *International Covenants on Human Rights,* (United
   Nations 1967).
8. E. Luard, *Human Rights and Foreign Policy* (Pergamon
   Press 1981) p. 20.
9. See, e.g., N. Daniels 'Equal Liberty and Unequal Worth
   of Liberty' in *Reading Rawls* (Blackwell 1975) ed. N.
   Daniels.
10. J. Madeley, *Human Rights Begin With Breakfast* (Pergamon
    Press 1982) pp. 2-4.

* * *

Chapter 4

1. If the *Brandt Report* is right, the assumption here is
   mistaken: avoiding protectionism may very well promote
   our interests. See Chapter 6 for discussion of this.
2. For a general discussion of 'social justice', see e.g.,
   D. Miller *Social Justice,* Clarendon Press 1976.
3. See B. Ward 'Disarm against a sea of troubles',
   Development Forum, Vol. 1, No. 1, 1973.
4. See in particular the section on 'Rejection of
   International Obligations' in Chapter 8.
5. J. Rawls, *op. cit.* Chapter 1 gives a useful summary of
   a long book.
6. J. Rawls, *op. cit.* pp. 60-61.
7. See J. P. Sterba, *The Demands of Justice* (University of
   Notre Dame Press, 1980) for an independent application
   of Rawls' method.
8. C. R. Beitz, 'Justice and International Relations',
   Philosophy and Public Affairs, No. 4, 1975, pp. 360-
   389, gives an international interpretation of Rawls'
   approach and argues for a 'global difference principle'.
   See also *The Brandt Report,* p. 32.
9. See J. Barry 'Do countries have moral obligations?' in
   The Tanner Lectures on Human Values, Volume II, ed. S. M.
   McMurrin (University of Utah Press and Cambridge U.P.
   1981) for a similar line of argument to this chapter.

* * *

1. Much of the material of this chapter has grown over many years of reading books and papers. Had I more time, I would have documented it much more fully. (Though even if I had, those unhappy with the approach would probably question the value assumptions in the documentation.)

2. L. Tolstoy, *What Then Must We Do,* (1886), Chapter 16.

3. This point illustrates an important fact that birth control programmes *without* adequate development and a sense of security will not be very effective. 'Development is the best pill'. See L. R. Brown, *In the Human Interest* (Pergamon 1974) for a useful discussion of population issues. See also F. Miller and R. Sartorius 'Population Policy and Public Goods', *Philosophy and Public Affairs* No. 8, 1979, for a perceptive discussion of motivation.

4. For detailed criticisms of Western Practices, see, e.g., T. Hayter, *The Creation of World Poverty* (Pluto Press 1981), S. George, *How the Other Half Dies* (Pelican 1976).

5. See, e.g., M. Muller, *The Baby Killer* (War or Want 1974)

6. See, e.g., J. Madeley, *Human Rights Begin With Breakfast* (Pergamon Press 1981),

7. *The Brandt Report,* pp. 218-220.

8. This represents an approach which seems to be fairly widespread. It is *a* 'conservative' approach, not *the* 'conservative' approach. Many of those who have a conservative approach are concerned about development, but are in fact highly critical of Aid or typical measures of economic planning. See, e.g., P. T. Bauer, *Dissent on Development* (Weidenfeld & Nicolson 1971). Even Bauer though is critical of the moral basis for Aid: see p. 126.

9. See, e.g., (apart from other radical works already mentioned) A. G. Frank *Crisis: in the Third World* (Heinemann Educational 1981) and other writings, C. R. Hensman, *Rich Against Poor* (Allen Lane, The Penguin Press 1971) for a radical critique.

10. See D. Hume *Enquiry Concerning the Principles of Morals,* ed. L. A. Selby-Bigge (Oxford 1902) p. 194, for a succinct criticism: "Render men's possessions ever so equal, men's different degrees of art, care, and

industry will immediately break that equality".

11. See, e.g., J. Bhaqwati, *The Economics of Underdeveloped Countries* (London 1966), p.36.
12. It is the emphasis on the 'sins of commission' rather than the 'sins of omission' which makes the character of works like *The Creation of World Poverty* rather different in tone from this work.

* * *

Chapter 6

1. *The Brandt Report*, e.g. p. 20 and passim.
2. *The Brandt Report*, e.g. p. 33.
3. *The Brandt Report*, e.g. pp. 46-7.
4. R. Higgins, *The Seventh Enemy* (Pan Books 1980), especially Part II.
5. R. Higgins, *op. cit.*, Chapter 12.
6. *The Brandt Report*, p. 64.
7. See 'Caring and Self-Fulfilment' in Chapter 11.

* * *

Chapter 7

1. See note (3) in Chapter 5.
2. See, e.g. J. Jerome, *Families of Eden - Communes and the New Anarchism* (Thames and Hudson 1974), and P. Rivers, *The Survivalists* (Eyre Methuen 1975).
3. The idea of 'appropriate technology' has been given powerful support in recent years by E. F. Schumacher in *Small is Beautiful* (Blond and Briggs 1973; Abacus 1974), though he used the phrase 'intermediate technology'. The periodical 'Appropriate Technology' is the publication of the Group which he founded, called the Intermediate Technology Development Group.
4. For a discussion of attitudes towards Nature, see, e.g., J. Passmore, *Man's Responsibility for Nature* (Duckworth 1974), and T. Derr, *Ecology and Human Liberation* (W.S.C.F. Vol. III, No. 1, 1973).
5. D. H. Meadows et al., *Limits to Growth*, Pan Books 1972. See also *A Blueprint For Survival* (The Ecologist and Penguin 1972).
6. See, e.g., M. Mesarovic and E. Pestel, *Mankind At the Turning Point* (Signet 1974); K. Sale *Human Scale* (Secker and Warburg 1980); *World Conservation Strategy*

(International Union for Conservation of Nature and
Natural Resources, (IUCN) 1980). See also R. Allen,
How to save the World (Kogan Page 1980; Corgi 1982),
which is based on the World Conservation Strategy.

7. See N. Dower, 'Ethics and Environmental Futures',
International Journal of Environmental Studies, Vol. 21,
No. 1, 1983, for an attempt to integrate an 'environmental ethic' into a common moral framework. See also
E. Ashby 'The Search for an Environmental Ethic' *Tanner
Lectures on Human Values,* ed. S. M. McMurrin (University
of Utah Press and Cambridge U.P. 1980) for a useful
discussion of the ethical issues raised by the environmental crisis.

8. See N. Dower 'Ethics and the Environment: some philosophical reflections on "The Just and Sustainable Society"',
Which Future for Scotland? ed. C. Pritchard, Church of
Scotland Home Board 1979, for further discussion of this
idea.

9. See also, e.g., J. Taylor *Enough is Enough* (SCM Press
1975).

* * *

Chapter 8

1. The character of this chapter is slightly unusual: it
represents a kind of inner dialogue which has been going
on in my thoughts over some years. If one is concerned,
as I am, with world poverty and environmental problems,
the question whether there is a dilemma involved is a
worrying one.

2. For further discussion of this idea, see notes (7) and
(8) in Chapter 7.

3. See, e.g., G. Hardin, 'Living on a Lifeboat' *Bioscience*
24, (1974), and 'Lifeboat Ethics - the Case against
Helping the Poor' *Psychology Today* 8 (1974). The latter
is reprinted in *World Hunger and Moral Obligation* ed.
W. Aiken and H. La Follette (Prentice-Hall 1977).

4. See O. O'Neill, 'Lifeboat Earth' *Philosophy and Public
Affairs* 4 (1975), p. 290. This is reprinted in *World Hunger
and Moral Obligation* (see note (3)).

5. I recall that Lord Caradon once used the thought-
provoking phrase 'the obligation of optimism'.

6. See, e.g., J. D. B. Miller 'Morality, Interests and

Rationalisation', in *Moral Claims and World Affairs*,
ed. R. Pettman, (Croom Helm 1979). See also R. B.
Brandt, 'Ethical Relativism', *The Encyclopedia of
Philosophy* Vol. 3, Ed. P. Edwards (Collier Macmillan
1967) for a survey of relativist views, which support
this position.
7. For this 'Hobbesian' view of International Relations
    see H. Bull, *The Anarchical Society* (Macmillan 1977)
    pp. 24-27 and elsewhere. The book contains much material
    on differing conceptions of international relations and
    world order.
8. The idea has a long history, and goes back to the
    arguments of Gorgias in Plato's *Gorgias* and of
    Thrasymachus in *The Republic* (Plato himself argued
    against these views).
9. For a discussion of the problems of affluence, see, e.g.,
    E. F. Schumacher, *The Age of Plenty* (St. Andrew Press
    1974), E. Fromm, *To Have or To Be?* (Jonathan Cape 1978
    and Abacus 1979), K. Sale, *Human Scale* (Secker and
    Warburg 1980).

* * *

Chapter 9

1. *The Brandt Report*, p. 14.
2. Lord Noel-Baker has been a life-long campaigner for
    disarmament. His book *The Arms Race* (London 1958) is a
    classic statement of the case. (I have been unable to
    find the location of the quotation itself.)
3. See, e.g., *The Brandt Report*, Chapter 7, J. Ferguson,
    Disarmament The Unanswerable Case(Heinemann 1982)
    Chapter 5, D. Skene, *Development and Disarmament*
    (Scottish Churches Action for World Development 1982),
    Bombs for Breakfast (Committee on Poverty and the Arms
    Trade 1978).
4. *The Brandt Report*, p. 16.
5. See, e.g., J. Ferguson, *op. cit.*, *Common Security*
    (Report of the Palme Commission : Pan Books 1982);
    J. A. Joyce, *The War Machine* (Hamlyn 1981).
6. See, e.g., *Nuclear Weapons and Christian Conscience*,
    ed. W. Stein (Merlin Press 1961).
7. Quoted in J. Ferguson *op. cit.*, p. 6.
8. D. Eisenhower, quoted in *The Coracle*, No. 2, Iona
    Community, 1980.

9. J. Harris, *Violence and Responsibility* (Routledge and Kegan Paul 1980), Esp. Chapter 2. cf. T. Honderich, *Violence for Equality* (Penguin Books 1976) pp. 152-4 and elsewhere. The five essays in this book contain much thought-provoking discussion on Violence.
10. J. Harris, *op. cit.*, p. 19.
11. QPAC, a group of Quakers travelling round the U.K. doing formal and informal education work on the theme of campaigning for a less violent world, is sponsored by Quaker Peace and Service, Friends House, Euston Road, London.
12. The approach is indicated by many expressions such as institutional repression, structural evil, etc. See, e.g., J. Harris, *op. cit.*, Chapter 3 (which includes quatations from Marx and Engels), P. Wolff 'On Violence' *Journal of Philosophy* No. 66 (1969) pp. 601-616 C.f. A. Curle, *True Justice* (Quaker Home Service 1981) p. 18. 'Liberation Theology' incorporates much of this way of thinking.
13. J. Ferguson, *op. cit.*, Chapter 4.
14. *The Brandt Report*, p. 13.
15. J. MacQuarrie, *The Concept of Peace* (Harper and Row 1973).
16. The connection between peace and 'true' justice is explored by A. Curle, *True Justice* (Quaker Home Service 1981).

* * *

Chapter 10

1. Oxfam is a well-known Third World Charity: others include UNICEF, Christian Aid, CAFOD, War on Want, Save the Children Fund. The World Development Movement is concerned with promoting public awareness of the Third World and applying political pressure on governments. Traidcraft (India House, Carliol Square, Newcastle NE1 6TY) markets Third World Crafts and also promotes tea and coffee: a percentage of the profits go to Third World workers.
2. J. S. Mill, *Utilitarianism* (e.g. in *Utilitarianism* ed. M. Warnock (Fontana 1962), Chapter 5, pp. 304-5.
3. See, e.g., J. Madeley, *Human Rights Start With Breakfast* (Pergamon Press 1982), Chapter 2.

4. Bishop M. Conti at a meeting of One World Week, Aberdeen, October 1978.
5. See, e.g. R. M. Hare, *Language of Morals* (Clarendon Press 1952) and *Freedom and Reason* (Clarendon Press 1963).
6. A rather different but useful account of caring is given in M. Mayeroff, *On Caring* (Harper and Row 1971).
7. See, e.g., R. Johann 'Love and Justice' in *Ethics and Society,* ed. R. T. de George (Macmillan 1968).
8. For an interesting documentation of various forms of social and personal transformation, see, M. Ferguson, *The Aquarian Conspiracy* (Routledge and Kegan Paul 1981 and Granada 1982).
9. See, e.g., *Religious Values and Development,* ed. K. P. Jameson and C. K. Wilber (Pergamon Press 1980) for discussion of the ways in which different religions can significantly support development.

* * *

Chapter 11

1. It is worth noting that if 'ought' implies 'can', the 'can' does not depend only upon the possession of a skill and the presence of external opportunity, but also significantly, if more subtly, on inner attitudes.
2. R. Higgins, *The Seventh Enemy* (Pan Books 1980) p. 221.
3. E. Fromm, *Man For Himself* (Routledge and Kegan Paul 1949), esp. Chapter 2, and *The Art of Loving* (Harper and Row 1956).
4. E. Fromm, *To Have or to Be?* (Jonathan Cape 1978 and Abacus 1979).
5. T. Nagel, *The Possibility of Altruism* (Clarendon Press 1970) esp. Chapters 3 and 9.
6. I. Kant, *The Moral Law* (trans. H. J. Paton: Hutchinson 1948) p. 96.
7. T. Nagel, *op. cit.,* Chapter XI.
8. See, e.g., N. Dower 'Ethics and the Environment: Some Philosophical Reflections on 'The Just and Sustainable Society'', *Which Future For Scotland?,* ed. C. Pritchard, (Church of Scotland Home Board, 1979), pp. 44-49.
9. R. M. Hare *Freedom and Reason* (Clarendon Press 1963), esp. Chapter 5 entitled 'Backsliding'.
10. F. H. Bradley, *Ethical Studies* (Oxford U.P. 1876) pp. 177-181.

11. For a sympathetic examination of the U.N., see E. Luard, *The United Nations* (Macmillan 1980).

SELECTED BIBLIOGRAPHY

Books on world issues raised in this book:

Brandt Commission, *North-South*, Pan Books 1980
Ferguson, J., *Disarmament The Unanswerable Case*,
  Heinemann 1982
Fromm, E., *To Be or To Have?*, Jonathan Cape 1978;
  Abacus 1979
George, S., *How the Other Half Dies*, Penguin Books 1976
Higgins, R., *The Seventh Enemy*, Pan Books 1980
Luard, E., *The United Nations*, Macmillan 1979
Madeley, J., *Human Rights Begin with Breakfast*,
  Pergamon Press 1982
Passmore, J., *Man's Responsibility For Nature*,
  Duckworth 1974.
Sale, K., *Human Scale*, Secker and Warburg 1980
Schumacher, E. F., *Small is Beautiful*, Blond and Briggs
  1973; Abacus 1974
Sider, R., *Rich Christians in an Age of Hunger*,
  Hodder and Stoughton 1978
Taylor, J., *Enough is Enough*, S.C.M. Press 1975
Ward, B. and Dubois, R., *Only One Earth*, Penguin Books 1972

Books on applied philosophy relevant to these issues:

Aiken, W. and La Follette, H., ed., *World Hunger and Moral
  Obligation*, Prentice-Hall 1977
Harris, J., *Violence and Responsibility*, Routledge and
  Kegan Paul 1980
Honderich, T., *Violence for Equality*, Penguin Books 1976
Singer, P., *Practical Ethics*, Cambridge U.P. 1979
Tanner Lectures on Human Values, Vol. I and II, ed. S. M.
  Mcmurrin, University of Utah Press and Cambridge U.P.,
  1980 and 1981

Books on general ethics:

Finnis, J., *Natural Law and Natural Rights*, Oxford 1980
Frankena, W., *Ethics* (2nd Edition), Prentice-Hall 1973
Fromm, E., *Man for Himself*, Routledge and Kegan Paul 1949;
  1975
Mackie, J. L., *Ethics*, Penguin Books 1977
Mill, J. S., *Utilitarianism*, e.g. Fontana Edition ed.
  M. Warnock, 1962

Nagel, T., *The Possibility of Altruism*, Oxford 1970
Rawls, J., *A Theory of Justice*, Harvard U.P. 1971

Some relevant Periodicals:

Development Forum, a U.N. Publication, Geneva 10,
    Switzerland
New Internationalist, 62a High Street, Wallingford,
    Oxon OX10 OEE
New World, publication of United Nations Association,
    3 Whitehall Court, London, SW1A 2EL
Philosophy and Public Affairs, Princeton U.P.
Spur, publication of World Development Movement, Bedford
    Chambers, Covent Garden, WC2E 8HA.

Action, 125, 127, 137, 150, 157 and attitude, 135, 139, and omission, 20ff, 70, 129-130
Affluence, *passim*, 2-3, 8, 33, 66, 83, 84, 87, 88, 98, 111, 116, 129, 144, 160
Africa, 53
Agribusiness, 57
Agriculture, 55
Aid, *passim*, 3, 39, 41, 43, 57, 61, 67, 73-77, 117, 134-136, 141 as international income tax, 5, 44-45
Altruism, 61, 155-157 *see also* benevolence, caring, charity
Animal Rights, 86, 136
Appropriate technology, 57, 83, 85, 169
Arms Race, 115-122
'As much as you can' doctrines, 19-20, 22, 25, 143
Attitudes, *passim*, 3, 31, 78, 80, 101, 102, 104, 122, 129, 130, 137, 149 of caring, 18, 80, 154, of openness, 23, 78, 146
Autonomy, 58, 62, 93, 94, 147

'Back to Nature', 84-89
Basic needs, 42ff, 94
Beneficiary of evil, 144
Benevolence, 22, 37-40, 43, 140, 145
Bentham, J., 14
Bias, 34
Birth control, 83, 90, 168
Blame, 68, 70
Bradley, F. H., 162
Brandt Commission Report, iii, iv, 5, 10-11, 57, 58, 64, 71-72, 73, 98, 115, 120, 130
Brotherhood of man, 30, 161
Bureaucracy, 8, 41 freedom from, 92

Capacity, to help, 32, 51-54, 102, 150-151 to promote good, 28
Capital-intensive methods, 57, 62, 73, 83
Capitalism, *passim*, 6ff, 41, 55, 56, 60, 62, 126
ring, 18, 32-33, 38, 148-149, 151, 160, 163 and self-fulfilment, 154-157 concept of, 145-147 society, 4-5, 42-43, 65, 93
Cause, evaluative meaning of, 42, 54, 118-119 of world poverty, 41-42, 55-59, 70
Centrally planned economy, 8, 9, 60, Charity, 5, 6, 30, 37-40, 43, 44, 67, 138, 145, 158
Choice, 31, 85, 137, 139-142, 145, 159
Christianity, 29, 34, 44 morality, 106, 158 theology, 161

Collapse, global, 10, 63, 72, 77-80
Collective, future, 90 madness, 122, obligation, 51 responsibility 4, 68, 133-135
Colonialism, 56-57, 60, 68, 127
Commitment, 3, 12-13, 28, 82, 99, 139, 141
Commodity prices, 71, 126
Communist approach, 6, 7, 55, 63 countries, 53 governments, 8, 127, 128
Community, 10, 85, 86, 105, 110 *see also* internationalism
Compassion, 10, 11 *see also* benevolence, caring, charity
Compensation, 68-70
Concept of Peace, The, 131
Conditions necessary for a reasonable life, 24-25, 31-32
Conscience, 34, 143-145, 160 salving, 7, 133, 144
Consequences, 18, 20, 22, 51, 54, 62, 119, 123, 127
Conservation, 89-91
'Conservative' approach, 5-6, 59-62
'Considered judgment', 18
Contraception, 60
Contractarian Theory, 28, 46
Co-operation as basis of morality, 3-5, 28, 102
Courage, 78-80, 122

Defence, 115ff
Democracy, 8, 46ff, 65, 92, 126, 131
Deterrence, 103, 118
Development, *passim*, meaning of, 73-74, 110-111, 164-165
Dialogue, North-South, 10, 72
'Difference Principle', 46-49
Disarmament, 103, 120-122
Discrimination, 49, 65, 67, 127
Disengagement, 62-63, 85, 91, 144-145
Distributive Justice, 64, 93
'Double Effect', doctrine of, 23
Duty, *passim*, not to kill, 20-23 beyond duty, 39, 158

Economics, *passim*, reform, 3, 7, 12, 59, 72 principles of fair dealing, 4, 41, 56-57, 93
Education, 1, 31, 32, 35, 45, 48, 55, 85, 116, 117, 138, 140, 151
Egalitarianism, 49-50, 64-66 directional, 65
Egoism, 15, 33, 61, 88, 146, 147, 154-157
Eisenhower, D., 121, 122
Energy, 83, 90, 110, 113
Engagement, 91, 144
Environment, 79, 83-94

Envy, 50
Ethical Studies, 162
Evil, 2, 42, 66, 67, 70, 127, 128, 144, 151
Experience, moral, 152, 160-163
Exploitation, *passim,* 40-41, 56ff, 69, 130, 147

Family, 17, 30, 31, 32, 111
Ferguson, J., 128
Finiteness of world, 89, 95
Food, 2, 57
Freedom and Reason, 158
Freedom/liberty, 19, 32, 35-36, 46, 48, 92 of religious expression, 25, 36, 92 of speech, 25, 92 political, 36, 147
Free Market, 9
'Free Rider', 76-77, 81
Friendship, 17, 30, 31, 32
Fromm, E., 34, 154, 160
Future, 17, 30, 89-90, 94, 99, 160

Gap between rich and poor, 2, 51, 64-66, 100, 101
Global, breakdown/crisis, 10, 63, 72, 77-80, 99, 100-105 conservation strategy, 89-91, 103 identity, 61, 77-80, 118, 160
God, 'That of God', iv., 30
Good, human, *passim,* 3, 14ff, 29ff elements of human, 31, 153 objective, 15-16, 29-30, 147
Government, policies, 44, 117-118, 133 pressure on, 129, 137-138 oppression, 127, 129, 131, 138
Growth, 83, 90, 95, 108-114

Happiness, 14, 29, 110, 154 Greatest Happiness Principle, 14
Hare, R. M., 158
Harm, inflicting, 125-127 preventing, 16, 20ff
Harris, J., 20-21 124-125, 129
Help, *passim,* meaning of, 11-12, 39, 52, 54, 59, 61 ways of helping, 12, 137-139
Higgins, R., 72, 152
Honderich, T., 20
Hope, 39, 78
Human Rights, *see* Rights

Ideal/idealism, 11, 28, 37, 51, 63, 77, 79, 100, 150-151, 157-158, 162
Identity, global, 61, 77-80, 160-161
Indifference, 36, 63, 69, 70, 120, 129-130, 144, 146, 163
Individual, role of, 80-82, 135ff
Individualism, 56
Inequalities, 47-48, 49, 64-68
Inflicting harm, 125-127

Injustice, 65, 68-69, 73, 127, 143-145, 147 *see also* justice
Institutional violence, 126-129
Intention, 22-23, 52, 54, 125-127
Interdependence, 4, 103, 106
Interest, national, 60, 79, 106-108, 120-122 longterm, 79 *see also* self-interest
Internationalism, 61, 80, 105, 118, 121, 148, 162-163 community/society, 3-5, 43, 79-80, 101-102, 118, 131, 152 co-operation, 101, 103 institutions, 9, 39, 102, 105, 162 law, 9-10, 27, 35 morality/obligation, *passim,* 4, 11, 43, 49, 91, 100-108, 161 pressure, 129 perspective, 9, 122 relations, 44, 100, 126 *see also* global, world
Involvement of West in Third World, 52ff, 88
Isolationism, 85

Justice, *passim,* and rights, 18, 37, (*see also* rights) and social minimum, 43-44 corrective, 64, 68-69 distributive, 64-66, 93 global society, 43-44, 49, 93-94 international, 43-44 'just and sustainable society', 91-94, 96 'justice not charity', 37, 158 'just war' 21, 120 love and justice, 147-148 principles of, 19, 40-50, 91-93 promoting, 142-145. social justice, 4-5, 10, 42-50, 93, 95-96, 100, 131

Kant, I., 155
Killing, 124 'The Arms Race Kills', 115-120 extension to omissions, 20-23
Kindness, 19, 37-40, 145 *see also* benevolence, caring, charity
Knowledge, 116, 140, 151, 153

Latin America, 53
'Left', the, 6ff, 43
Liberal approach, 46ff, 93, 127
Liberation struggles, 127-129
Liberties, *see* Freedom, Rights
Life, conditions of reasonable, 24-25, 31-32 expectancy, 2 right to, 3, 24ff, 93
Life-style, simple, 84-85, 87-88
Limits to Growth, 89
Love, 34, 131, 145 love and justice, 147-8 *see also* caring
Luard, E., 35

MacNamara, R., 1
MacQuarrie, J., 131
Madeley, J., 36
Man for Himself, 154

Marxism, 6, 41, 63-64, 126, 127
Materialism, 81, 86, 149, 154, 160
Material possessions, 33, 49
Maximin policy, 47
Maximisation, of good, 15, 18, 28
   of interests, 33, 75-76
Means and ends, 11-13, 22, 128, 138,
   155
Medicine, 55
Metaethics, 166
Militarism, 64, 118, 131
Mill, J. S., 14, 140
Minimum, socio-economic, 43-44, 45, 93
Minority groups, 8, 18, 49, 58
Missionaries, 52
Monoculture, 57
Morality, *passim*, and self-interest,
   74-77, 122, 159-160 Christian, 106
   conceptions of, 2-4, 28-29, 88,
   141-142 consciousness, 22, 86, 135,
   141, 148, 152, 157 experience, 152,
   157, 160-163 living morality, 162
   'moral point of view', 15 'moral
   space', 19-20, 33 objectives, 90,
   135, 138-145, 158 objectivity, 113
   rights, 26-29 (*see also* rights)
   scheduling of priorities, 30, 117
   use of moral argument, 5-8
Motivation, 51, 60, 150-152, 157-158,
   161
Multinational companies, *passim*, 10,
   41, 56-58, 62, 73, 83, 133

Nagel, T., 155
National Interest, *see* interest
Nationalism, 34, 66
Nature, 'Back to Nature', 84-89
   reverence for, 86
Negative responsibility, 22-3, 29
New International Economic Order,
   10, 41, 57, 133, 164
Noel-Baker, P., 115
'No growth' policies, 83, 90, 109,
   111
Non-Violence, 128
North-South Dialogue, 10,72
Nuclear war, 72, 79, 100
Nuclear weapons, 120-122

Objective value, 155-156
Obligations, *passim* international,
   100-108 imperfect, 140
Omission, 20ff, 66, 70, 129-130 sins
   of, 68, 130, 169
OPEC, 56
Openness, 78, 145, 148-149, 157, 163
Oppression, 65, 126-129, 138 of min-
   ority groups, 58
Optimism, 78-80, 104-105, 122, 150,
   170
'Original Position', 46ff

'Ought', 38, 42, 109, 135, 142, 148,
   158, 173
Overstatement, use of, 115, 122-123

Pacifism, 21, 120, 128
Peace, 130-132, 136
Personal relationships, *see* relation-
   ships
Persuasion, 5-7, 113, 137
Pessimism, 104-105, 122
Philosophy, iii, 14, 25, 50, 97,
   142, 166
Pleasure, 14, 30, 33-34, 111, 116,
   146, 147, 154
Pollution, 64, 89
Population crisis, 56, 83
Possibility of Altruism, The, 155-156
Poverty, absolute, *passim,* 1-2, 24,
   41, 90, 94, 100
Practical solipsism, 155-156
Prejudice, racial, 68
Prescriptivism, 158
Present, the, 99
Pressure on governments, 129, 137-138
Preventing harm, 16, 20ff
Principles, 139-145 of justice, 40-
   50, 91-93
Promoting, good, 3, 14, 51, 102, 146,
   155 justice, 51, 142-145
Protectionism, 12, 41-42, 58, 71,
   76, 81
Prudence, 78, 122
Punishment, 18 international, 68-69

Quaker, iv., 30, 115, 120 Peace Action,
   Caravan, 125, 172
Quality of life, 20, 34, 55, 65, 84,
   86-87, 111, 152, 160, 163

Racialism, 34, 66-68
Radical, conception of violence,
   124ff new radicalism, 8 'radical'
   approach, 6-7, 62-64
Rationality, 5-7, 15-16, 155 rational
   agents, 46, 155
Rawls, J., 45-49, 92
Realism, 100
Reason to act, 20, 148, 155
Recycling of resources, 110, 112
Redistribution, 7-8, 66, 93
'Reflective Equilibrium', 166
Reforming approach, 7, 10
Regulation of economy, 8
Relationships, personal, 20, 32, 86,
   110, 123, 126, 147, 154
Relativism, 44, 105
Religious outlook, iii, 29, 149, 161
   see also Christian
Resources, natural, 2, 64, 72, 83,
   89-90, 95-97, 108-114 newly
   extracted, 110

Responsibility, *passim,* 11, 32-33, 61, 69-70, 123 collective, 68, 133 negative, 22-3, 129 sense of broad, 148-149, 157 society's, 42
Revolution, 6, 7, 62, 63-64, 128, 138
Rights, *passim,* and obligations, 25, 26, 107-108 institutional, 26-28, 34 moral/human/universal, 26-30, 131 natural, 29-30 to liberties, 18, 25, 35-36, 92 to life, 3, 24ff, 93, 122-123 to pursue interests, 33, 75, 106-108 United Nations Declaration, 26-27, 35-36
'Right', the, 5ff, 43
Rules, 15, 31, 134-135, 139-143, 147

Saving for future, 17
Schumacher, E. F., 9
Security, 118, 120-122, 130
Self-fulfilment, 34, 112, 154-157
Self-Interest, 5, 10, 30, 71ff, 154, 159-160 conceptions of, 78-9, 160 enlightened, 10, 73
Selfishness, 33, 63, 66, 129
Self-sacrifice, 19, 76
Self-sufficiency, 83, 88
Seventh Enemy, The, 72, 152
'Shalom', Hebrew concept of, 131
Sider, R., 2
Sins, of omission/commission, 68, 130, 169
Slave Trade, 60
Small is Beautiful, 9
Socialist approach, 6, 8, 48
Society, 91-94 *see also* international
South Africa, 66-67
Strategic interests, 53-54, 74
Subjective valuing, 20, 32
Supererogation, 20
Sustainable society, 91-94, 95-96, 99
Taxation, international, 5
Technology, appropriate, 57, 83, 85, 169 fix, 89
Theft, 122-123
Theology, 161
Theory of Justice, A, 45-49
Time, use of, 16
Timing, relevance of, 99
To Have or To Be?, 154
Tolstoy, L., 54
Trade, *passim,* boycott, 138 'terms of trade', 56, 'trade not aid', 39
Traidcraft, 172
Transnational, companies, *see* multinational, relationships, 3-5
'Trickle down' theory, 97
Trust, 78-80, 122

United Nations, 12, 35, 103, 105, 121, 161-162
Universalisability, 142

Utilitarianism, 14-20, 22, 28

Valuing, subjective/objective, 20, 146-147
'Veil of Ignorance', 46
Vertical and Horizontal, metaphor of 87, 91
Violence, 122-130 definitions of, 125 institutional, 126-129 negative, 126
Violence and Responsibility, 20-21, 124-125
Violence for Equality, 20-21

Wages, low, 25, 56, 61, 144
War, 70 accidental, 121 fighting in, 124 just, 120
Ward, B., 10-11, 43-44
Welfare state, 43, 93, 127
West, the, *passim,* attitudes, 66 governments, 58, 60, 133-135 involvement, 54-59, 62-63, 88
World, Bank, 9, 12, 58 citizenship, 79, 80, 162 economy, 62 government, 9 *see also* global, international